MAINTAINING A
WordPress
SITE USING
HTML & **CSS**

The Advanced Guide

First Edition

The Website Series #3

Shere L.H. McClamb, Ph.D., PMP, PMI-ACP, ITIL

First published: March 2020

Published by The bITa Group
Publishing@TheBitaGroup.com
Benson, North Carolina 27504

ISBN: 978-0-578-64572-8

Preface

Welcome to Maintaining a WordPress Site Using HTML & CSS: The Advanced Guide, the third of The Website Series of books. **In *Building a Website Using WordPress: The Beginner's Guide,*** you learned that WordPress is built on the LAMP *(Linux, Apache, MySQL, Php)* Stack and how to build your site from the ground up using all open source tools. In ***Making Your WordPress Site Awesome - The Intermediate Guide,*** you learned to enhance the site by employing accessibility, security, and engagement strategies. The goal of ***Maintaining a WordPress Site Using HTML & CSS: The Advanced Guide,*** is to move you from the role of WordPress web site designer to WordPress web site developer! The skills you have amassed as a WordPress site owner gives you the foundation required to go under the hood of the WordPress site and make some real magic.

In **Maintaining a WordPress Site Using HTML & CSS: The Advanced Guide**, we will focus on the structure: HTML and the design elements: CSS of the WordPress site and the countless ways it can be manipulated to create a more robust experience. Many will ask: is another HTML/CSS book REALLY needed? My answer is of course, yes! To me, it is not the content but the style in which those who are new to the language need it presented. I find that a majority of students are not looking to code an entire site using only code. Most are using some GUI website tool to do the heavy lifting and want the ability to understand and manipulate the code when needed. Let's face it, as good as front-end applications are, having a working knowledge of the language the pages are created in is a major plus.

HTML has had such a short but tumultuous history. The most difficult part of writing this book was balancing how much of HTML5 I should include for the absolute beginner of HTML and CSS and a veteran of WordPress. My goal is to supply a firm foundation to move forward and use HTML and CSS to build and maintain your WordPress sites, but it is tempting to take you down memory lane and include deprecated tags, and how DOCTYPES have evolved. You will notice that I do include information from older versions of the language for reference.

Who is this book for?

- **Individuals** who are visual WordPress Gurus who want to use HTML and CSS to enhance their experience.
- **Instructors** who are tasked with teaching beginner HTML and CSS to WordPress veterans.

Conventions

The following conventions are used to walk you through building a web site using HTML and CSS:

- Step-by-step methodology.
- Using open-source resources.
- Tips around known pitfalls that may hinder progress.

What this book covers

About the Author

Shere L.H. McClamb has more than 21 years working in the Information Technology field in the roles of Business Intelligence and Business Systems Analyst, IT Project Manager, Webmaster, Instructional Technologies Developer, and Technologies Instructor. She has taught at community and 4-year colleges as well as working for various governmental agencies within the State of North Carolina.

Shere holds a Ph.D. in Information Technology from Capella University, develops websites and print media for her wonderful clients, teaches Web technologies to adults, and currently works full-time as a Business Systems Analyst for the North Carolina State Bureau of Investigations in Raleigh, North Carolina.

Thanks

To my family and friends for all of their love and support!

Table of Contents

MODULE ONE

UNDER THE WORDPRESS HOOD

CHAPTER ONE: THE WORDPRESS SITE - UNDER THE HOOD

> *You have conquered the WordPress platform user interface and you are yearning for more. Under the Hood will definitely scratch that itch by exploring the components, structure, design and construction of pages and posts.*

In this chapter, you will:

- Essential Elements
- The Structure
- Background Files
- Content Types

Now that you are a WordPress visual editor professional, it is time to dig deeper into what makes the platform one of the most popular content managers in the world. To do this, it is essential to understand how the WordPress site is constructed and how all the components fit together to construct the website. Every WordPress theme uses the exact same framework components to build a site, it is up to the developer to make it unique. Knowing what the technologies are and how to use them is the key to your continuing success!

THE ESSENTIAL ELEMENTS

The essential elements of every WordPress site:

Hyper Text Markup Language

A language that uses markup to describe the structure of Web pages. The basic building block of all websites.

Hypertext Preprocessor

HTML-embedded Web scripting language. This means PHP code can be inserted into the HTML of a Web page. When a PHP page is accessed, the PHP code is read or "parsed" by the server the page resides on.

Cascading Style Sheets

A style sheet language used for describing the presentation of a document written in a markup language.

Images

JPEG, PNG, GIF, etc.

THE STRUCTURE

WordPress themes are created using a folder of template files, each of which controls a specific piece of your theme.

config-bbpress . File folder	**config-events-calendar** File folder	**config-wpml** File folder	**css** File folder
framework File folder	**images** File folder	**includes** File folder	**js** File folder
lang File folder	**404.php** PHP File 840 bytes	**archive.php** PHP File 1.21 KB	**footer.php** PHP File 3.55 KB
forum.php PHP File 1.78 KB	**functions.php** PHP File 8.82 KB	**functions-incarnation.php** PHP File 17.5 KB	**header.php** PHP File 6.10 KB
index.php PHP File 680 bytes	**page.php** PHP File 1.28 KB	**screenshot.png** PNG image 32.3 KB	**search.php** PHP File 1.00 KB
searchform.php PHP File 328 bytes	**sidebar.php** PHP File 4.83 KB	**single.php** PHP File 2.07 KB	**single-sermon.php** PHP File 1.99 KB
style.css Cascading Style Sheet Document 1.39 KB	**template-archives.php** PHP File 4.49 KB	**template-blog.php** PHP File 1.53 KB	**template-dynamic.php** PHP File 2.38 KB
template-post-timeline.php PHP File 1.85 KB	**template-sermon.php** PHP File 1.54 KB	**wpml-config.xml** XML Document 2.28 KB	

Accessing and Reviewing Your Site's Root Files

All of the files for your WordPress site theme reside in your wp-content root folder. The steps outlined should look familiar. If you need a refresher on how to access and work with theme files, refer to *Building a Website Using WordPress: The Beginner's Guide* there are 2 in-depth chapters on this very topic.

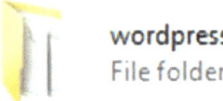

wordpress
File folder

The content of this folder performs very different tasks and are very important, especially during the maintenance of the web site. Let's look at the contents of the WordPress press package:

Name	Type	Size
wp-admin	File folder	
wp-content	File folder	
wp-includes	File folder	
index.php	PHP File	1 KB
license.txt	Text Document	20 KB
readme.html	Chrome HTML Do...	8 KB
wp-activate.php	PHP File	5 KB
wp-blog-header.php	PHP File	1 KB
wp-comments-post.php	PHP File	5 KB
wp-config-sample.php	PHP File	3 KB
wp-cron.php	PHP File	4 KB
wp-links-opml.php	PHP File	3 KB
wp-load.php	PHP File	4 KB
wp-login.php	PHP File	34 KB
wp-mail.php	PHP File	9 KB
wp-settings.php	PHP File	11 KB
wp-signup.php	PHP File	25 KB
wp-trackback.php	PHP File	4 KB
xmlrpc.php	PHP File	3 KB

FOLDERS (DIRECTORY)

wp-content is where your themes that control the way your site looks and the plugins that extend functionality of the site are located.

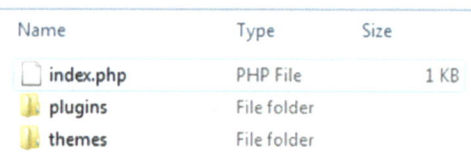

wp-includes are the workhorse files, these php files tells your site what to do, how, and when to do it.

certificates	category-template.php	class-wp-customize-manager.php
css	class.wp-dependencies.php	class-wp-customize-nav-menus.php
fonts	class.wp-scripts.php	class-wp-customize-panel.php
ID3	class.wp-styles.php	class-wp-customize-section.php
images	class-feed.php	class-wp-customize-setting.php
js	class-http.php	class-wp-customize-widgets.php
pomo	class-IXR.php	class-wp-editor.php
SimplePie	class-json.php	class-wp-embed.php
Text	class-oembed.php	class-wp-error.php
theme-compat	class-phpass.php	class-wp-http-ixr-client.php
admin-bar.php	class-phpmailer.php	class-wp-image-editor.php
atomlib.php	class-pop3.php	class-wp-image-editor-gd.php
author-template.php	class-simplepie.php	class-wp-image-editor-imagick.php
bookmark.php	class-smtp.php	class-wp-theme.php
bookmark-template.php	class-snoopy.php	class-wp-walker.php
cache.php	class-wp.php	class-wp-xmlrpc-server.php
canonical.php	class-wp-admin-bar.php	comment.php
capabilities.php	class-wp-ajax-response.php	comment-template.php
category.php	class-wp-customize-control.php	compat.php

Root-Level Files Explained

index.php

* Front to the WordPress application. This file doesn't do anything, but loads wp-blog-header.php which does and tells WordPress to load the theme.

 *license.txt

In the introduction we talked about navigating to the license files when determining whether a web site was WordPress driven? Well here it is.

```
WordPress - web publishing software

Copyright 2015 by the contributors

This program is free software; you can redistribute it and/or modify
it under the terms of the GNU General Public License as published by
the Free Software Foundation; either version 2 of the License, or
(at your option) any later version.

This program is distributed in the hope that it will be useful,
but WITHOUT ANY WARRANTY; without even the implied warranty of
MERCHANTABILITY or FITNESS FOR A PARTICULAR PURPOSE.  See the
GNU General Public License for more details.

You should have received a copy of the GNU General Public License
along with this program; if not, write to the Free Software
Foundation, Inc., 51 Franklin St, Fifth Floor, Boston, MA  02110-1301  USA

This program incorporates work covered by the following copyright and
permission notices:

   b2 is (c) 2001, 2002 Michel Valdrighi - m@tidakada.com -
   http://tidakada.com
```

readme.html – See below!

wp-activate.php

* Confirms that the activation key that is sent in an email after a user signs up for a new blog matches the key for that user and then displays confirmation.wp-blog-header.php*

wp-blog-header.php

* Loads the WordPress environment and template. *

wp-comments-post.php

* Handles Comment Post to WordPress and prevents duplicate comment posting. *

wp-config-sample.php

* The base configuration for WordPress. The wp-config.php creation script uses this file during the installation. You don't have to use the web site, you can copy this file to "wp-config.php" and fill in the values. *

wp-cron.php

* WordPress Cron Implementation for hosts, which do not offer CRON or for which
 * the user has not set up a CRON job pointing to this file. * *Basically used for scheduled jobs.*

wp-links-opml.php

* Outputs the OPML XML format for getting the links defined in the linkadministration. This can be used to export links from one blog over to another. Links aren't exported by the WordPress export, so this file handles that. *

wp-load.php

* Bootstrap file for setting the ABSPATH constant and loading the wp-config.php file. The wp-config.php file will then load the wp-settings.php file, which will then set up the WordPress environment. *

wp-login.php

* WordPress User Page. Handles authentication, registering, resetting passwords, forgot password, and other user handling. *

wp-mail.php

* Gets the email message from the user's mailbox to add as a WordPress post. *

wp-settings.php

* Used to set up and fix common variables and include the WordPress procedural and class library. *
 * Allows for some configuration in wp-config.php*

wp-sign-up.php

* Sets up the WordPress Environment. *

wp-trackback.php

* Handle Trackbacks and Pingbacks Sent to WordPress *

xmlrpc.php

// Some browser-embedded clients send cookies. We don't want them.

Using the Notepad++ Text Editor

This is a text file and will need to be opened in a text editor. Notepad++ is a free text editor. Navigate to https://notepad-plus-plus.org/

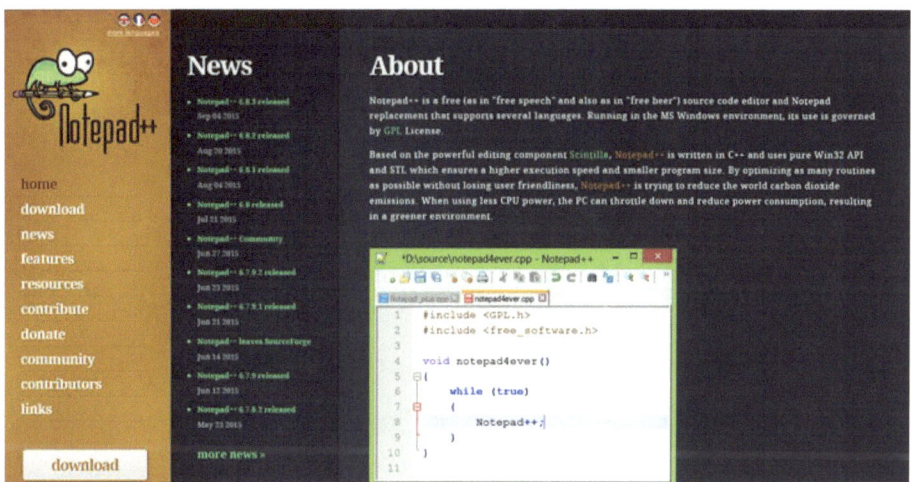

Step 1.   Click on the "download" link or button.

Step 2.   When the download screen appears, click the oval download button.

Step 3.   The file will download to your computer.

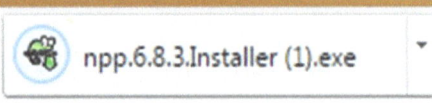

Step 4.   Choose the language.

Step 5.   Click the "Next" button to work through the installer instructions.

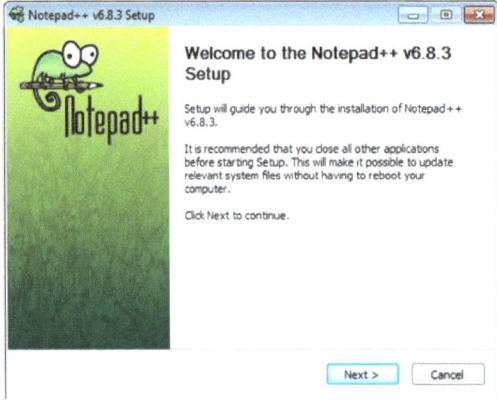

Step 6.   Accept the Terms of Agreement by click on the "I Agree" button.

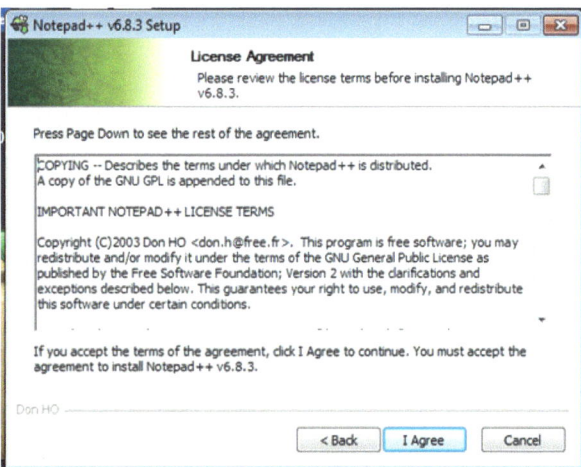

Step 7.   You will probably not need to alter the destination folder.

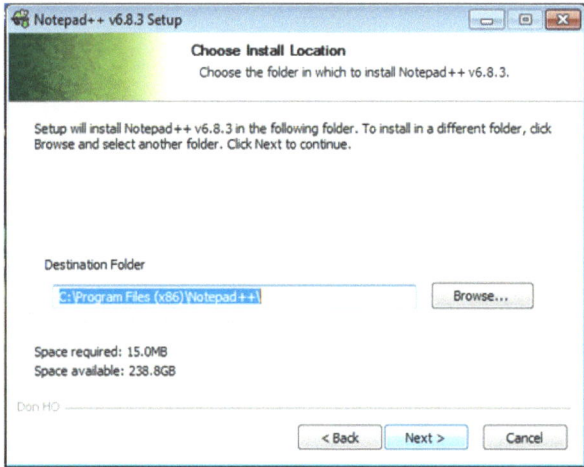

Step 8.   You are fine with the components that are check by default.

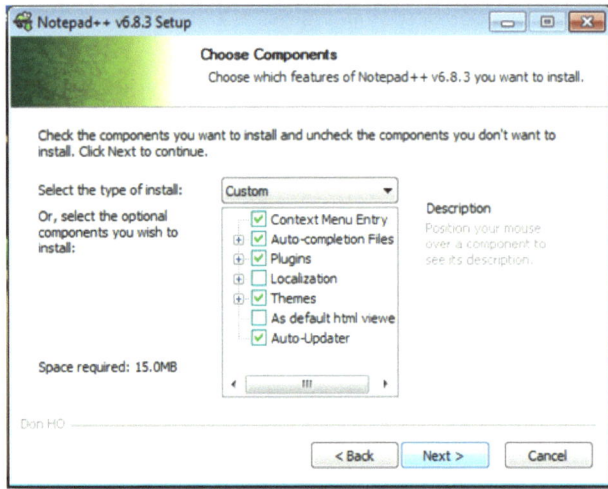

Step 9.   ONLY check the option to place a shortcut on your desktop

Step 10.   Click on the "Install" button.

Step 11.   Click the "Finish" button

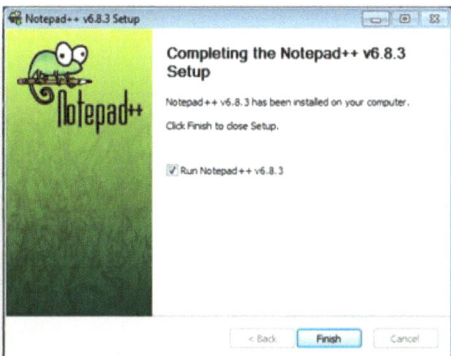

Step 12.   Open Notepad++

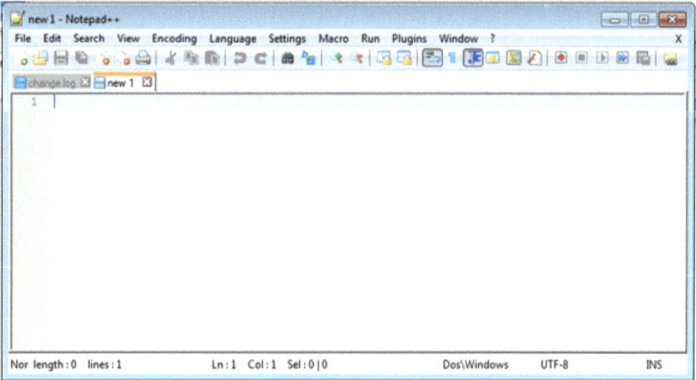

15

CONSTRUCTION OF THE HOMPEPAGE

When you visit the home page of a WordPress site in your web browser, the HTML will call up these two PHP files. Then, these files will call up additional files to construct the WordPress site dynamically. WordPress is dynamic in the way that it assembles pieces of content for the purpose on constructing pages made of very specific content. Since WordPress runs primarily on PHP, the home page is actually created using several different files.

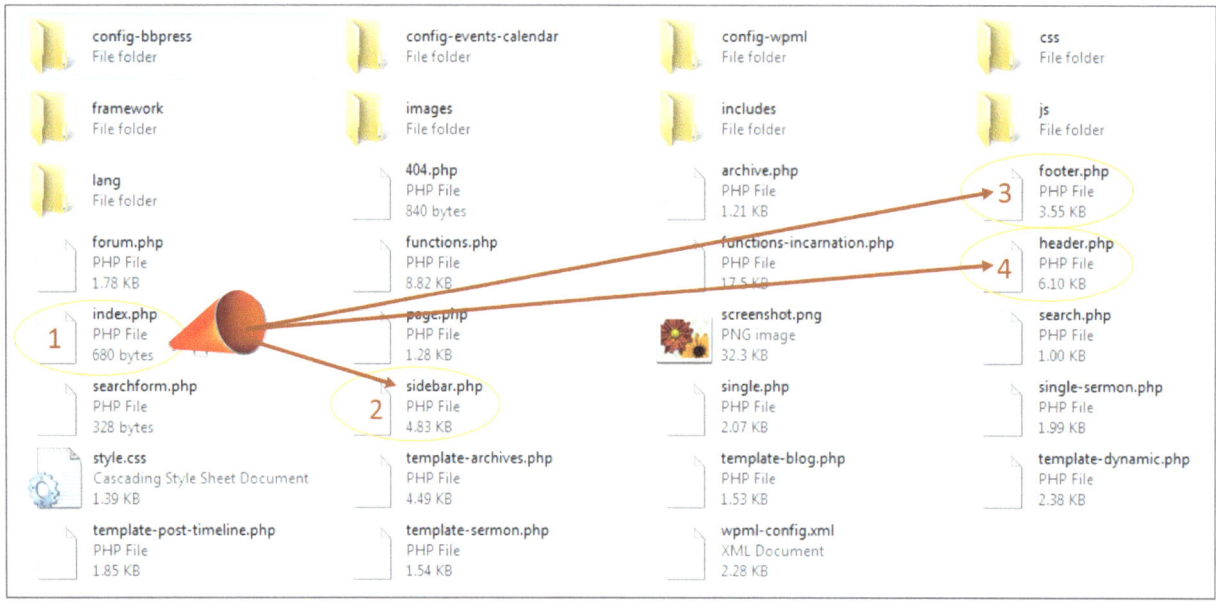

The **index.php** file, tells the header, sidebar, and footer where to appear on the page and each of these subsequent files tells the browser what content to display in those areas.

The **header.php** file, brings up the content (site name and menus) you want to appear in the top section of the homepage.

The **sidebar.php** file, calls up the sidebar portion of the theme, which is where most people place their social media stuff, site categories, recent posts, recent comments, etc.

The **footer.php** file, calls up the footer portion of the site.

The Index File

The **index.php – home** file controls what the homepage of your WordPress theme looks like. By default, it is a loop that queries and then displays the most recent blog posts, with a link in the bottom to view previous posts. Using options in the WordPress Dashboard you can have the homepage point to post or page you created.

WP Dashboard -> Settings -> Reading -> Reading Settings

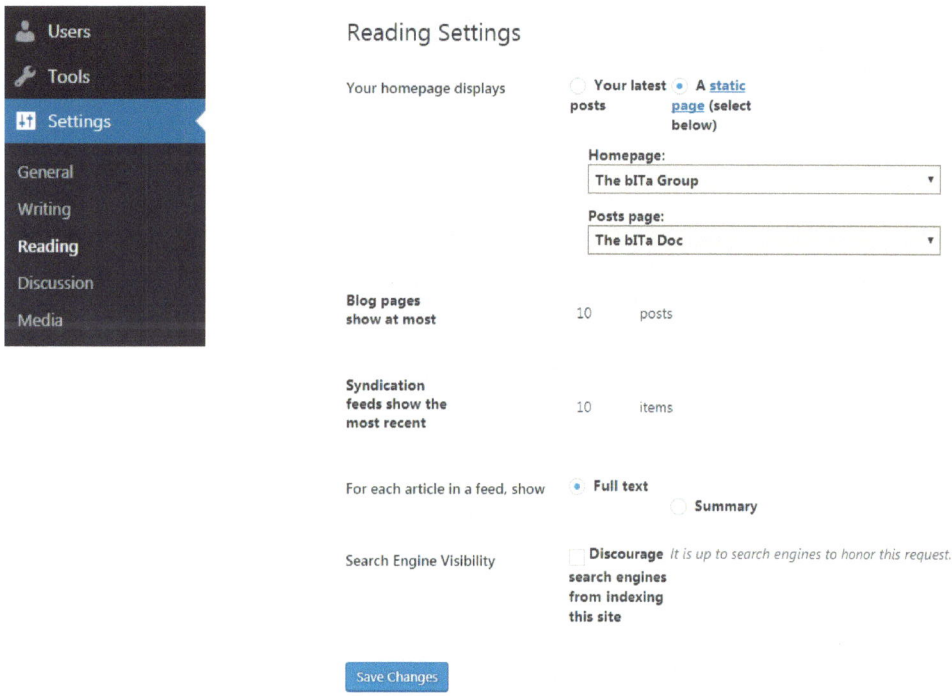

In this case, you will specify the page, post or URL for the regular blog posts to appear on, and that page is generated by index.php.

The Header File

The **header.php** file is global. It that contains HTML code and displays headers and navigation.

```
header.php - Notepad
File  Edit  Format  View  Help
<?php

# Looking for the header content? You'll find it inside "header-default.php"

/*
        This page is meant to catch plugins that try loading content outside the design making direct calls to "the_header()" and "the_footer()"
        we start by turning on output buffering to capture the output attempting to display
*/

ob_start();

/*
        Now we skip to "footer.php" and finish capturing the output before returning to the theme to display it properly
*/

?>
```

The Single File (Posts)

The **single.php** file parses and displays **individual posts** by querying in the loop. On most WordPress themes, the attributes for individual posts are carried in the single.php file. When you click on the "Read more," link on the teaser for a post on the homepage of a blog, you'll be taken to that individual post. While you can have many posts on a site, how they look, and function are determined by the single.php file. It's a basically a template.

```
single.php - Notepad
File  Edit  Format  View  Help
<?php

if (__FILE__ == $_SERVER['SCRIPT_FILENAME']) { die(); }

/*
 * NOTE: this file is for compatibility.
 * Layouts are created in the theme options and "design-{name}.php" files.
 * Content is generated by the "template-{context}.php" files.
*/

create_page_layout('post');     // context = post

?>
```

- Posts encourage conversation
- Posts are timely
- Posts are social
- Posts can be categorized
- Posts are included in RSS feed
- Posts do not have custom template feature

The Page File

The **page.php** file allows for the display of individual pages and controls what pages look like. The same can be said for individual pages. You know, your "About Me", "Contact", and other static pieces of content? Page attributes are carried by the page.php file.

```
page.php - Notepad
File  Edit  Format  View  Help
<?php

if (__FILE__ == $_SERVER['SCRIPT_FILENAME']) { die(); }

/*
 * NOTE: this file is for compatibility.
 * Layouts are created in the theme options and "design-{name}.php" files.
 * Content is generated by the "template-{context}.php" files.
 */

create_page_layout('page');      // context = page

?>
```

- Static "one-off" type content
- Pages are timeless
- pages are hierarchical
- Pages are not meant to be social in most cases
- A dated feature called "order" which lets you customize the order of pages by assigning a number value to it.
- Pages are not included in the RSS feed
- Timeless content is considered to be more important

The Sidebar File

Using the **sidebar.php** file allows for the inclusion of sidebars on the page and if you want it to look different than the other pages on the site.

```
sidebar.php - Notepad
File  Edit  Format  View  Help
<?php

// This file servers no purpose other than being a placeholder.
// It's here so that you don't get junk WP content if a rogue plugin makes a random call to "get_sidebar()"
```

Custom Page Templates

Creates custom page templates using your theme.

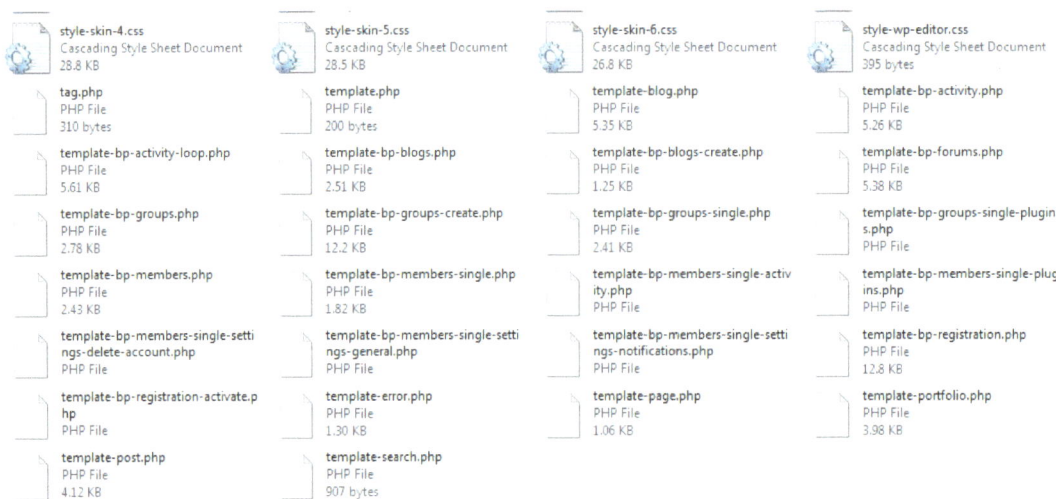

The Loop

The display of contents of the main area of your site are controlled by individual WordPress theme template files using what's called "the loop".

Query post or page

Start Loop
      the_title (outputs the title of the post)
      the_excerpt (outputs the post excerpt)
      the_content (outputs the full post content)
      the_category (outputs the post categories)
      the_author (outputs the post author)
      the_date (outputs the post date)
      other tags (there is a variety of other tags you can use in the loop)
      endwhile;
Exit the loop

The loop is perhaps the most powerful part of your WordPress theme. It starts with a query (which determines which posts or pages to grab) and ends with a PHP "endwhile" statement. Everything in-between is up to you. You can specify the output of titles, post content, metadata, custom fields and commenting all within the loop, each element is output for each post or page until the query is done. You can set up multiple loops and queries on a single page; for example: on a single.php you could have the loop showing the entire content of a single post, with a loop outputting just titles and thumbnails for related posts below it.

The Archive File

archive.php

The Category File

category.php

```
category.php - Notepad
File  Edit  Format  View  Help
<?php

if (__FILE__ == $_SERVER['SCRIPT_FILENAME']) { die(); }

/*
 * NOTE: this file is for compatibility.
 * Layouts are created in the theme options and "design-{name}.php" files.
 * Content is generated by the "template-{context}.php" files.
*/

create_page_layout('category'); // context = category

?>
```

Taxonomies, sort your content, improve the usability, content by topic

http://yoursite.com/**category**/analytics/

- broad grouping of your posts
- encompass a group of posts
- table of contents for your site
- hierarchical, so you can sub-categories
- There are no SEO benefits to adding multiple categories.

21

The Tag File

tag.php – archives

```
tag.php - Notepad
File  Edit  Format  View  Help
<?php

if (__FILE__ == $_SERVER['SCRIPT_FILENAME']) { die(); }

/*
 * NOTE: this file is for compatibility.
 * Layouts are created in the theme options and "design-{name}.php" files.
 * Content is generated by the "template-{context}.php" files.
 */

create_page_layout('tag'); // context = tag

?>
```

Taxonomies, sort your content, improve the usability, content by topic

http://yoursite.com/**tag**/food/

- describe specific details of your posts
- site's index words
- micro-categorize your content
- not hierarchical
- not required to add any tags

You can control the look and feel of different archives using template files also. If there is no archive file, the archives will look like index.php; however, you can create an archive.php to override that. If you create a file called category.php, it will override archive.php for categories only. If you create a tag.php, you can override it for tag archives only.

The Sidebar File

The **sidebar.php** file displays, you guessed it, the sidebars. Multiple sidebars can be set up in functions.php, and contents of sidebar widgets are set up from the WordPress wp-admin panel.

```
sidebar.php - Notepad
File  Edit  Format  View  Help
<?php

// This file servers no purpose other than being a placeholder.
// It's here so that you don't get junk WP content if a rogue plugin makes a random call to "get_sidebar()"
```

The Footer File

The **footer.php** file contains instructions for global footer and closes HTML tags.

```
footer.php - Notepad
File  Edit  Format  View  Help
<?php global $designBypassContent;

# Looking for the footer content? You'll find it inside "footer-default.php"

/*
        This page is the second part in catching plugins that try loading content outside the design making direct calls to "the_header()" and "the_footer()"
        Previously in "header.php" we turned on output buffering to capture the output. Now we will return that content and load the theme design.
*/

$designBypassContent = ob_get_clean();

/*
        Last thing... load the theme design normally and it will detect the content of "$improperLoadContent" and add it to the output.
*/

create_page_layout('page');      // context = page

?>
```

BACKGROUND FILES OF A WORDPRESS THEME

In order for a WordPress theme to work, it needs a few essential background files. These files can be modified to your needs and can quite powerfully affect the custom look and functionality of your site.

The Comments File

The **comments.php** file controls the output of comments, which can be included in the loop if you desire comments on your theme. Comments.php can be overridden by plugins such as Disqus, which then take over comment functionality on your blog.

```
comments.php - Notepad
File  Edit  Format  View  Help
<?php
// Do not delete these lines
if (!empty($_SERVER['SCRIPT_FILENAME']) && 'comments.php' == basename($_SERVER['SCRIPT_FILENAME']))
        die ('Sorry, you can\'t load this page directly. ');
?>

<!-- Post Comments -->
<div class="userComments" id="Comments">
        <div id="comments" class="hidden"></div>

        <?php
        if ( post_password_required() ) {
                echo '<p class="nocomments">';
```

The Functions File

The **functions.php** file allows you to put your own custom PHP code in order to modify core elements of your theme. It is often used to specify multiple sidebars, change the number of characters in the excerpt or add custom admin panel options for wp-admin.

The Search File

If the theme you're using has the option of adding a search box (which they all do), the search results will appear thanks to **search.php**.

The Comments File

And if someone makes a boo-boo when typing in an address or a link is broken, that'll be handled by 404.php. Can you guess what **comments.php** controls? Yup. The comments section on each post is handled by this file.

```
404.php - Notepad
File  Edit  Format  View  Help
<?php

if (__FILE__ == $_SERVER['SCRIPT_FILENAME']) { die(); }

/*
 * NOTE: this file is for compatibility.
 * Layouts are created in the theme options and "design-{name}.php" files.
 * Content is generated by the "template-{context}.php" files.
 */

create_page_layout('error'); // context = error

?>
```

It's a pretty simple concept to understand when you get right down to it and every WordPress theme uses these bones and muscles to hold the structure of the site together. Without these elements, the site wouldn't exist in any usable sort of way. It'd just be a bunch of disparate components. A header floating here. A footer floating there. It'd be a headless, footless, beast of a thing and we definitely wouldn't want that!

DESIGN ELEMENTS

We're talking about CSS here it dictates how your WordPress theme looks. The CSS file controls the layout and design elements within those structural elements.

To put it more simply, while the PHP files control where the header shows up, the CSS tells it what size and font the text should be in that space, where images should appear, and if there should be any tables (and, if so, how large each cell should be). You get the idea.

All the content would appear in place, but it could still come off pretty drab. You know when a website breaks or is slow to render and the page has a white background, the font is Times New Roman, blue hyperlinks, and all the text is left-aligned...Yeah. That's what Web pages and WordPress themes would look without CSS. NOT PRETTY.

The Style Files

This is the main CSS stylesheet for your theme. It also contains text at the top which tells WordPress what the name of your WordPress theme is, who the author is and what the URL of your site is.

```
style-default.css - Notepad
File  Edit  Format  View  Help
/*** Primary Style Sheet for Theme ***/

/* Primary font family and color
-------------------------------------------- */
body, select, input, textarea {
   color: #6B7074;
   font-family: Arial, Helvetica, Garuda, sans-serif;
   line-height: 1.4;
}

/* Links
-------------------------------------------- */
a, a:active, a:visited  { color: #1f7099; }
a:hover                 { color: #d91a54; }

    /* box style links */
    .boxLink, #BP-Content .generic-button a                              { -webkit-border-radius: 2px;
-moz-border-radius: 2px; border-radius: 2px; font-size: .9em; }
    a.boxLink, a.boxLink:link, a.boxLink:visited,
    #BP-Content .generic-button a:link, #BP-Content .generic-button a:visited    { padding: 1px 5px 2px; color: #fff; background-color:
#1f7099; }
    a.boxLink:hover, a.boxLink:active,
    #BP-Content .generic-button a:hover, #BP-Content .generic-button a:active    { background-color: #d91a54; }

    /* "inContainer" links (Showcase, Call to Action, etc.) */
    .inContainer a, .inContainer a:active, .inContainer a:visited { color: #53A5CC; }
    .inContainer a:hover { color: #fff; }

    /* footer links */
    #Bottom footer a, #Bottom footer a:active, #Bottom footer a:visited { color: #ABB2B8; }
    #Bottom footer a:hover { color: #fff; }

/* Design styles
-------------------------------------------- */
/* Invisible areas for fade in effect on page load */
.invisibleMiddle #Middle,
.invisibleAll #Top, .invisibleAll #Middle, .invisibleAll #Bottom { visibility: hidden; }
.ie6 #Top, .ie6 #Middle, .ie6 #Bottom,
```

Similar things happen server-side for the categories and tags pages. Individual category pages are generated using category.php and archive.php and tags are handled by tag.php.

So, when you create new categories or new tags, they'll automatically be included on their respective pages, with all of their associated content included. Again, it's pretty cool to think how all of this happens when you click on a link. It's all disassembled content, and with one click, it's cobbled together.

WHERE TO USE HTML AND CSS IN WORDPRESS

The WordPress Text Editor

If you have upgraded to the newer versions of WordPress, you have noticed that in line with HTML%, they have introduced "blocks". I have found it better to switch to the Classic Editor to work with the source code editor. You can choose the classic editor on the Pages screen or you can choose to return to the classic editor once you are on the page.

Classic Editor

On the Pages screen, scroll to the page you wish to work with. Hoover over the page name and **click Classic Editor**.

    ☐   AUDIO/VISUAL MINISTRY — Block Editor
                Block Editor   Classic Editor   Quick Edit   Trash   View

Text Tab

You are now on the visual representation of the WordPress page. To go to the text editor, **click on the Text tab**.

                    Visual   Text

HTML/CSS Coding Area

The area starting at the cursor is where you will type of the new and exciting elements you are about to learn.

The WordPress Theme Editor

Click on **Appearance** in the Main left menu and then **click Theme Editor**

The **Theme Files** can all be updated. It is good practice not to code straight into your file, but instead make a playground (e.g. using a child theme) as a development and staging space.

MODULE TWO

HTML

HYPERTEXT MARKUP LANGUAGE

CHAPTER TWO: INTRODUCTION TO HTML

The goal now, is to get a foundational understanding of the HTML, the language of the Web. Understanding how web pages are constructed is the foundation of moving forward in understanding WordPress under the hood.

In this chapter, you will:

- A Brief History of HTML
- About the W3C
- How to Ensure Accessibility
- How HTML and CSS work together to make Web Pages

The HTML language has had a tremendous effect on the world in its short life span. Moving from its beginnings where the goal was to merely share documents among the world's scientists and large library collections being an integral part of everyday life for everyone all around the globe.

This chapter focuses on providing an overview of the work that goes on to support the language we all experience in our daily lives and how to make sure that the content of web space continues to be accessible to all of us regardless of our human limitations.

WHAT IS HTML?

HTML stands for **H**yper**T**ext **M**arkup **L**anguage.

The World Wide Web Consortium (W3C) defines HTML as:

> A language that uses markup to describe the structure of Web pages (https://www.w3.org/standards/webdesign/htmlcss).

A Brief HISTORY of HTML

Let's walk through a very brief history of HTML. This will give an appreciation for all of the great things this language can accomplish compared to its ground-breaking yet humble geek-centered beginnings. A name all of HTML junkies know Tim Berners-Lee as the Father of the Internet (more information can be found on https://www.w3.org/People/Berners-Lee/) Sir Berners-Lee wrote the first HTML code to share information using links in 1989, the prototype of early HTML was developed in 1992, and the rest as they say IS HISTORY!

HTML 5 2008	The latest version of HTML is version 5, which give HTML greater control using CSS and without the use of helper languages.				
	XHTML 1.0 2000	A reformulation of HTML in XML. It contains 3 DTD's defined in HTML 4.0.			
		HTML 4.01 1999	HTML 4.0 1997	4.0 was a major release, it wasn't until version 4.01 included support for CSS & forms.	
3.0 was the next version in development but was not release. The next major version release is HTML 3.2.			HTML 3.2 1997	HTML 3.0 1995	
The first version of HTML introduced and recommended.					HTML 2.0 1995

THE W3C

Formed in 1994, the World Wide Web Consortium, continues to oversee the open standards of the Web. Led by Tim Berners-Lee this consortium which continues to transform itself and the Web. The W3C consists of a number of companies, governmental agencies, professionals, and individuals who have a stake in the evolution of a strong open source Web for years to come. Defining HTML was the W3C's initial focus, but as time has passed this has come to define Cascading Style Sheets (CSS), Scalable Vector Graphics (SVG), The Web Open Font Format (WOFF), the Semantic Web stack, Extensible Markup Language (XML), and a variety of Application Program Interfaces (API). According to the W3C (www.w3C.com) the design should focus on usability goals, user characteristics, environment, tasks, and workflow as the user interacts with hardware, software, and websites.

Specifications and Guidelines

Technical specifications and guidelines presented by the W3C come out of the user-groups that have the boundaries and the growth of the Web as a major focus for their work and/or their industries. These guidelines not only pertain to HTML for web pages. It also involves setting guidelines for the formatting and scripting languages that are used to enhance HTML, browsers architecture of the Web, mobile devices, web services, and Web authoring tools. For more information on the specifications and guidelines presented by the W#C please visit the specifications wiki at https://www.w3.org/wiki/HTML/Specifications.

Recommendations and Standards

The W3C is not a regulatory body, rather, it consists of technology thought leaders who recommend a base Web standard for the Internet and for the language. For more information on the recommendations and standards presented by the W3C please visit their standards page at https://www.w3.org/standards/.

ENSURING ACCESSIBILITY

Accessibility refers to principals and guidelines for personal, business, and government websites that make web content such as text, images, and training materials more accessible to those with disabilities. The 508 Compliance Standards and Web Content Accessibility Guidelines WCAG are technical standards that outline the criteria for successfully developing websites that ensure accessibility for all.

Some guidelines are in line with good website design and you will comply without even realizing it. For instance, criteria for good navigation includes the ability of users navigating through a site know where they are and how to get to the information they are looking for. Users should also be able to understand site content, specifically as to the readability and characteristics of text and backgrounds. Content and formatting are separated by using HTML for the structure and CSS for formatting of the Web page. Many high priority compliance guidelines pertain to the creation of tables and forms.

Accessibility and WCAG 2.0

Web Content Accessibility Guidelines (WCAG) 2.0, guidelines to make website content more accessible was released in 2008 as an update to WCAG 1.0 released in 1999.

Clean HTML
This is of utmost importance when writing HTML, CSS, or PHP for your site.

Keyboard Support
Users should be able to move around the website using only the keys on their keyboard.

Text Alternatives for all Non-Text Content
W3C encourages authors to fill in information for media elements in their sites.

A Style-Free Option
Using fonts that are not 'works of art' to the point they would not be easily recognized by screen reading applications.

ARIA (Accessible Rich Internet Application)
Landmarks tell the assistive technology what it's reading, where they are on the page, and what to do next.

Color Contrast
Colors should have a sharp contrast and not close in color and hue.

Seizure-Inducing Graphics
Graphics that blink relentless without the ability for the user to turn them off should not be used.

Time-Limits
Limitations on the amount of time it takes for any action or reaction on the sire should be removed.

THE DOM

HTML PARSING

The browser reads the directions given by the HTML tags and attributes and builds a document object model (DOM) tree.

ALL TAGS ARE NODES

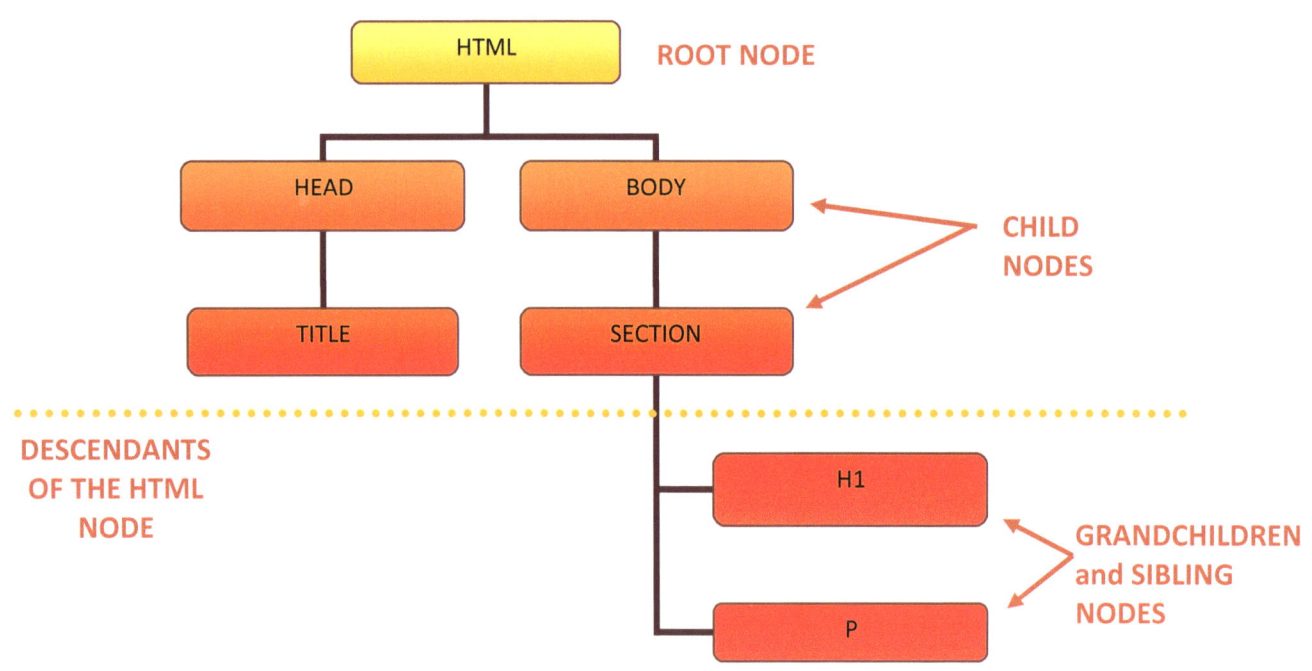

CHAPTER THREE: GATHERING YOUR SITE REQUIREMENTS

> *There are software and hardware requirements you will need in addition to a working knowledge of HTML and CSS to bring your web pages to the World Wide Web.*

In this chapter, you will:

- Learn about Domain Names
- Securing a Web Site Host
- Installing a Source Code Editor
- Installing and Configuring the FTP Client
- Working with your Web Site Directory

In this chapter, you will learn how to acquire the Web site authoring tools you need to create your first Web document. The tools of a Web Author include a domain name and Web space from a Web hosting company, applications for code editing and transferring files to your Web server, and of course your local computer (desktop, laptop, tablet, or phone).

INSTALLATION PREPRARATION

There are several items that need to be taken care of prior to installation:

Domain Name- Every Web page on the Internet resides under a domain name (somewhere.com) or an ip address (the name of a computer, a router, the owner and the name of the computer on the Internet).

Web Site Host- A company that brokers (sells) domain names, Web space, and other Web site related elements for a price.

Installation of a source code editor – Notepad++ will be the default Source Code Editor.

Installation of an FTP Client –FileZilla will be the default File Transfer Client.

Preparation of the Website Directory - The Web site files need to be moved to your local website folder. You will create the directory through your web host.

Create a FTP User - You need to create a user that will administer the transfer of files from the local and remote servers. You will create the directory through your web host.

DOMAIN NAMES AND WEB SPACE

There is information that is required for the FTP client to connect to your web server and for those on the Internet to access your Web site.

Selecting a great domain name is an important step towards a successful website. There are many credible websites that offer domain name registrations. It is often less stressful on those who are new to dealing with domains to purchase the domain name from the same vendor who will host your site. Hosting companies usually offer domain name and hosting together in a package. If you are new to purchasing a domain name, it is recommended to take time and due diligence in researching pricing and reputation of a hosting company prior to signing up. Many times, a discount or special pricing is given when a domain name is purchase bundled with web hosting space.

Top-Level Domains

Let's talk about (Top-Level) domain name extensions. Knowing the extension that best fits your website tells your users you are 'web-informed'. For example, dotcoms URLs ending in **.com** are so over and often incorrectly used.

We will cover the more popular ones:

      .com represents the word "commercial"

      .net represents the word "network"

      .org represents the word "organization"

      .biz is used for "small businesses"

      .info is for credible resource websites and signifies a "resource"

      .mobi is short for "mobile"

.tv is for rich content/multi-media websites, commonly used within the entertainment or media industry.

.travel is used for travel and tourism industry related sites

Your domain name should adequately represent your site content. Over the years there have been many naming schemes have come and gone, but URLs that represent their entities well have stood the test of time. What if the best domain name for you is already registered? With the popularity of the internet, your second or third best choice is probably the one that is going to be available.

Don't get discouraged – domain names can be up to 67 characters (including numbers and letters) so get creative!

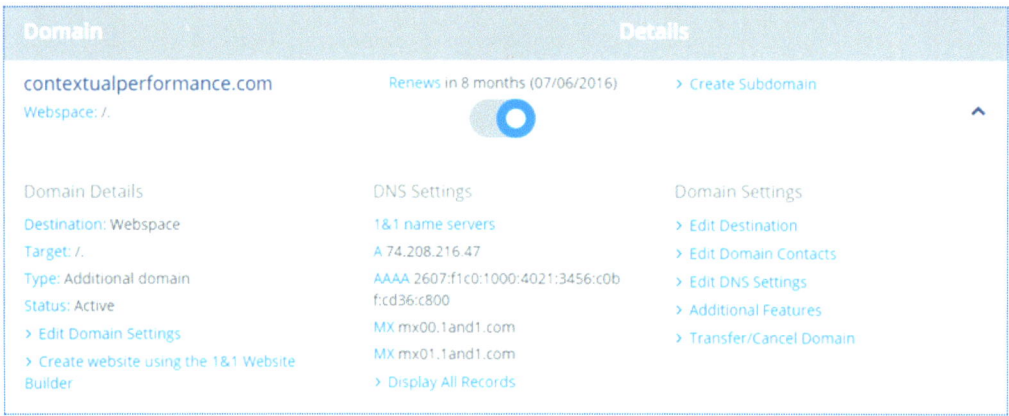

Securing a domain name is relatively easy and straightforward. There are several web hosts that register domain names.

Again, try to find and use the hosting company that best fit your needs by getting the most for your money. We discuss web hosts and what they provide in the next section.

WEB HOSTS

Choosing the right host for your website is important for the success of your website. A Web host is the company that houses and displays your website on demand for your visitors. Take the time to choose a hosting solution to best fit your requirements. The types of Web site hosting options commonly available are free, shared, virtual private server (VPS), dedicated, and managed Web Site hosting.

Web hosts will often offer solutions through packages charged monthly. These packages should include the features you will need to create a website.

- Web Space
- FTP (File Transfer Protocol) Access
- Traffic Volume
- Email Addresses

It is important that the hosting solution you choose has unlimited access to the elements required to install and maintain your website. It is also important for hosts to guarantee the data center that houses your site is secure and will run with as little interruption as possible. Limited downtime should be their #1 priority. The exact package you will require is based on the need of your website, so advance planning of your site will allow you make sound decisions in this area.

When Choosing a Hosting Service:

*Domain Name *(required)*
Most domain names are purchased from a web host. When choosing a web host, investigate the benefits of securing the domain name as part of securing the web hosting package. Many times, a generic domain name is included with the hosting package with an option to upgrade it to one of your choosing a special price.

*Web Space *(required)*

This is the space your website will take up on the hosts server. Host often divide a server into compartments of space and sell it to individuals on a monthly basis. Think of this as renting a home for your website. If you plan to have a lot of content (images, movies, music) you should plan to purchase more space than let's say a blogger who will mostly write articles containing mostly text. I understand, being new to this you probably have no idea how big your site will be or how much space you will need. Well, you can always buy more space – so no worries there.

FTP User Profiles *(required)*

Mostly all mid-tier hosting packages come with the ability to create FTP users. Web site files will be moved from your local computer to your web server via FTP (file transfer protocol).

Traffic Volume

There are many hosting packages to choose from. Make sure that your package can handle the amount of traffic you anticipate for your website. As you can see in the hosting examples provided the more popular hosts offer more space than you will ever use. Still take the time to ensure you have the right amount of space for your website needs.

Email Addresses

The email addresses supplied through your host will provide @YourDomainName for a professional and polished look.

Web Hosts

Below are just a few of the many web hosts available to choose from:

1&1

http://www.1and1.com/

Bluehost

http://www.bluehost.com/

Dreamhost

https://www.dreamhost.com/

HostGator

http://www.hostgator.com/

Inmotion Hosting

https://www.inmotionhosting.com/

Siteground

https://www.siteground.com/

NOTEPAD++ SOURCE CODE EDITOR

The HTML and CSS files will be created and edited in a text editor. Notepad++ is a free and open sourced text editor.

STEP 1.   Navigate to https://notepad-plus-plus.org/.

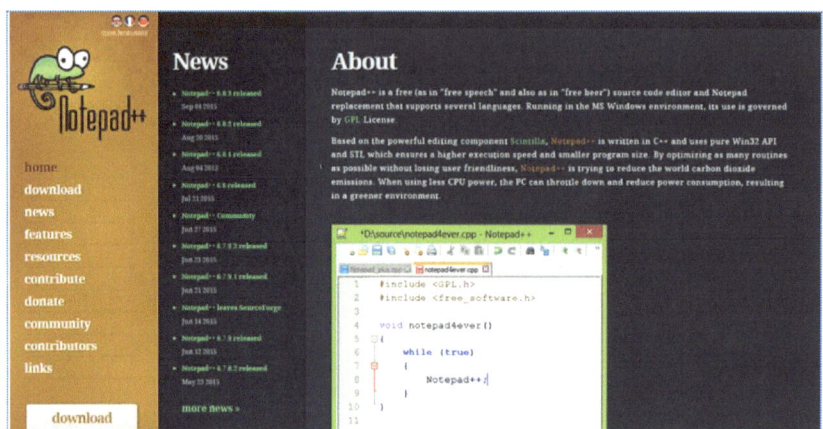

STEP 2.   Click the **download** link or button.

Result: The download screen appears.

STEP 3.   Click the oval download button.

Result: The file will download to your computer.

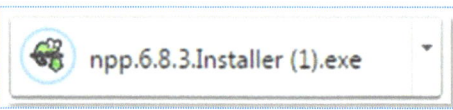

STEP 4.   Choose the language from the
dropdown menu.

STEP 5.   Click the **Next** button to work
through the installer instructions.

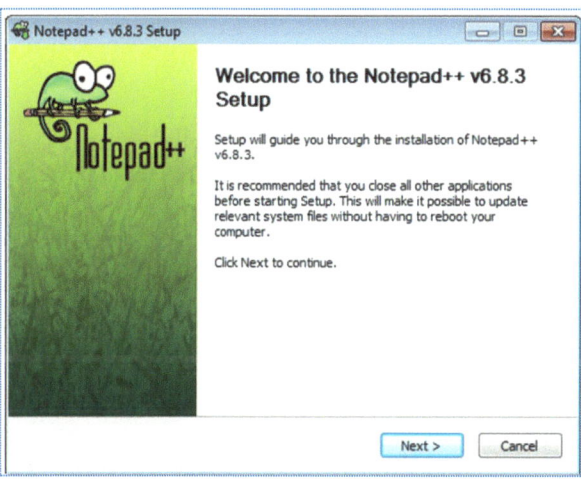

STEP 6.   Accept the Terms of Agreement by clicking on the **I Agree** button.

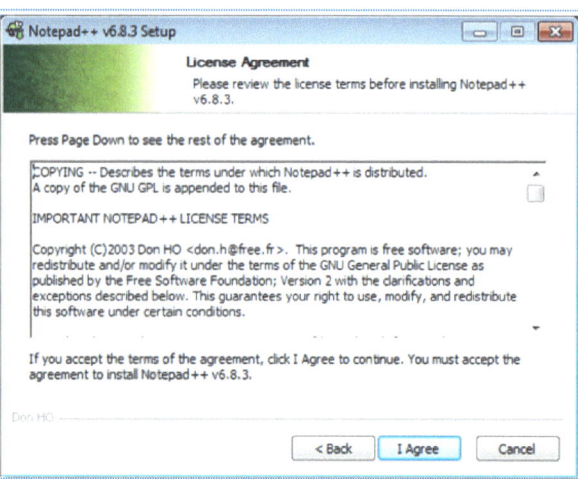

STEP 7.   You will probably NOT need to alter the destination folder.

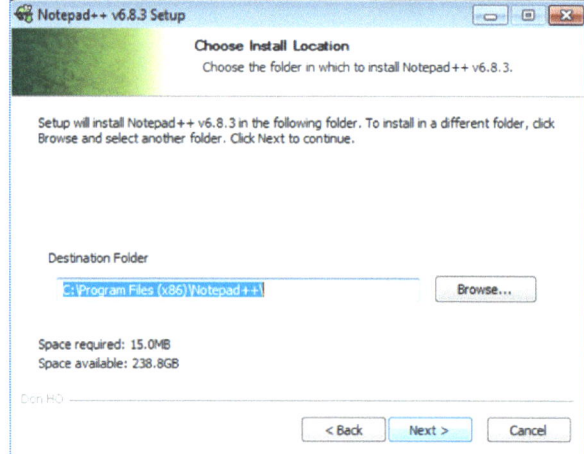

STEP 8.   It is good to start with the
            components that are checked by
            default.

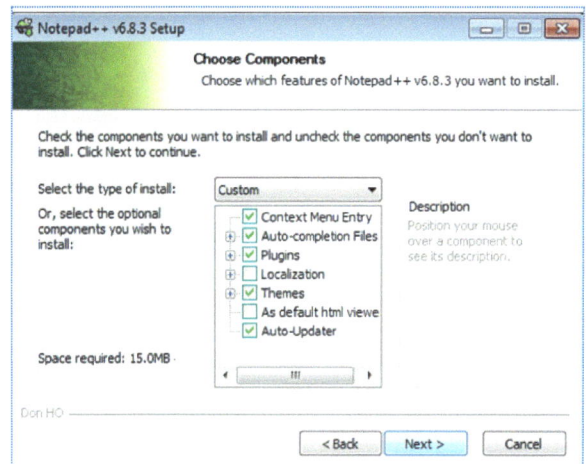

STEP 9.   ONLY check the option to place a shortcut on your desktop.

STEP 10.   Click the **Install** button.

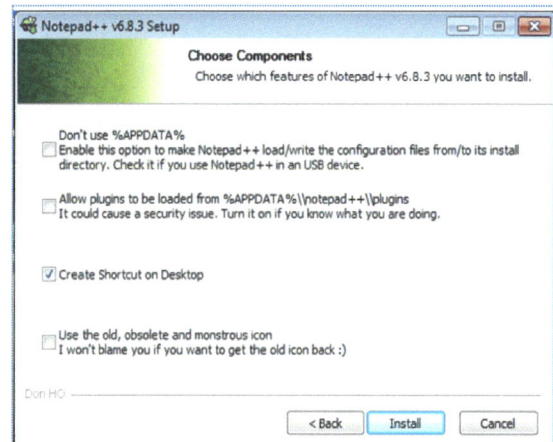

STEP 11.   Click the **Finish** button.

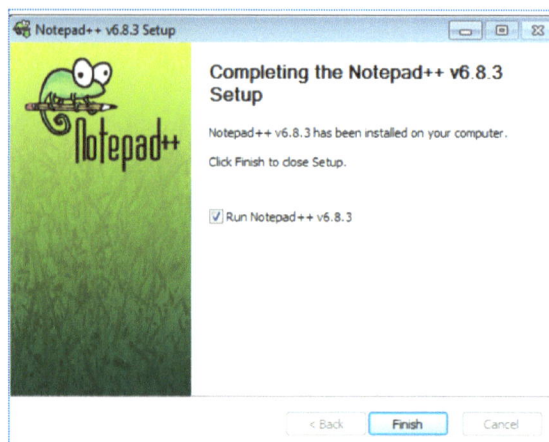

> **Result:** Notepad++ is now installed
> on your computer.

STEP 12.   Open Notepad++.

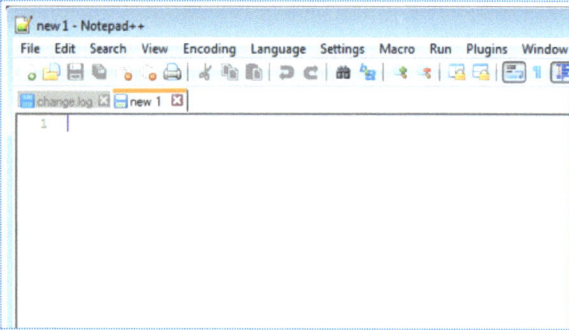

STEP 13. Create and save a
WebSiteInformation.txt to record
important information to be used
later in the installation process.

UPLOADING SITE FILES TO YOUR WEB SERVER

File Transfer Protocol (FTP)

This step in the process involves moving the files from your local computer to your web server. The process used to move files on the Internet is called the File Transfer Protocol (FTP). What distinguishes FTP from most other protocols is the use of secondary connections for file transfers.

There are two file locations that we will concern ourselves with:

Local Files

Local files are the files that live in the directories on your computer or thumb drive.

Remote Files

Remote files are the files that live on the web server.

When you connect to an FTP server, you are actually making two connections.

1. A control connection is established, over which FTP commands and their replies are transferred.

2. To transfer a file or a directory listing, the client sends a particular command over the control connection to establish the data connection.

The data connection will be established passive mode. Using passive mode, the client sends the PASV command to the server, and the server responds with an address. The client then issues a command to transfer a file or to get a directory listing and establishes a secondary connection to the address returned by the server.

Securing an FTP Account

Manage the connections to your webspace with an FTP username and password. This should be found in a section of your host's dashboard to manage your webspace.

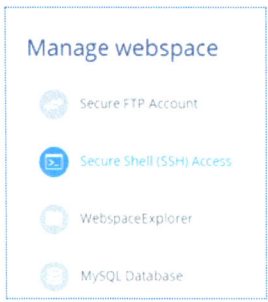

STEP 1.   Click the **FTP** option (Secure FTP Account).

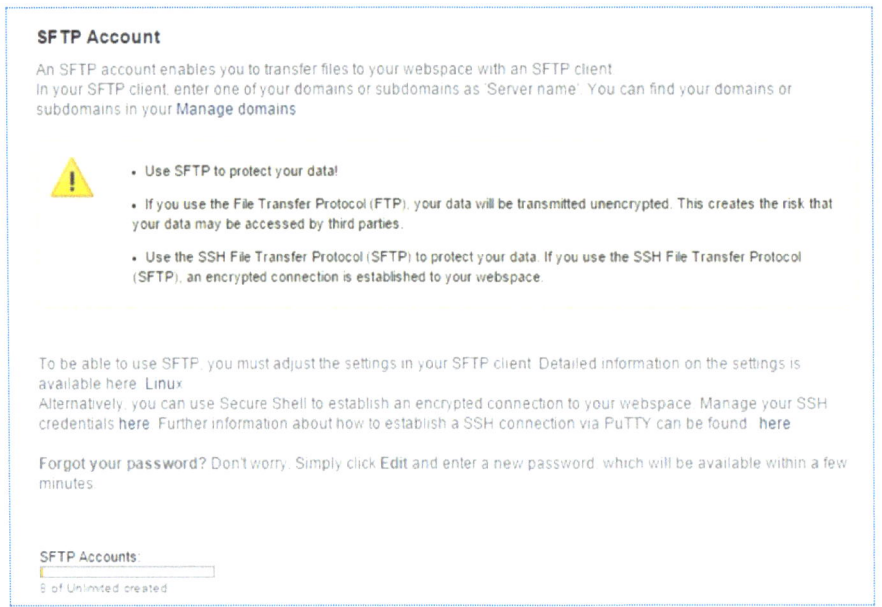

STEP 2.   Follow the instructions to create a new FTP User.

STEP 3.   Fill out the information to create a new FTP user.

STEP 4.   Remember, this information is case sensitive! Click the **Save** button.

Result: A FTP user account is created.

STEP 5.   Record all of the technical information in the Notepad++ document and save it as **Website Information.txt.**

FTP Clients

WinSCP {Windows} A free, open source FTP, SFTP, SCP and FTPS client known as the most powerful and easy to use FTP client for Windows users.

FireFTP {Windows | Mac | Linux} A free, secure, cross-platform FTP/SFTP client for the Mozilla Firefox browser. FireFTP is a Mozilla Firefox add-on, so the user experience is seamless because FireFTP blends into the web browser. You need the Mozilla Firefox browser to use it.

FileZilla {Windows} A popular free FTP clients for Windows that is available on all other platforms as well. It has been reported that adware and/or spyware was downloaded with the FileZilla download. You can uncheck the boxes during the installation to remove any extra functionality you may not need.

Transmit {Mac} The most popular FTP client for Mac, particularly among web developers. Transmit at a cost per license.

CyberDuck {Windows | Mac} Free and open source FTP, SFTP, WebDAV, Rackspace Cloud Files, Google Docs, Windows Azure & Amazon S3 software for use with Mac and Windows.

gFTP {Linux}
An open source FTP client for Linux-based operating systems.

INSTALLING THE FileZilla FTP CLIENT

STEP 1.   Navigate to the FileZilla main page - https://FileZilla-project.org/

STEP 2.   Click the **Download FileZilla Client** button.

STEP 3.   Click the **Download Now** button.

Result: The download should start automatically. If it does not, click the **Start Download** button.

STEP 4.   Once your download is complete, you will receive a thank you message. **Close this page.**

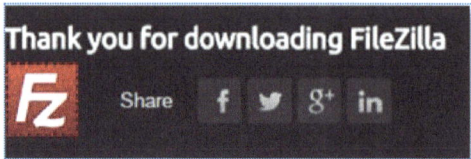

STEP 5.   Click on the zipped **executable** file. Options to run the file will appear.

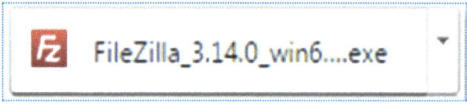

STEP 6.   Click the **Run** button.

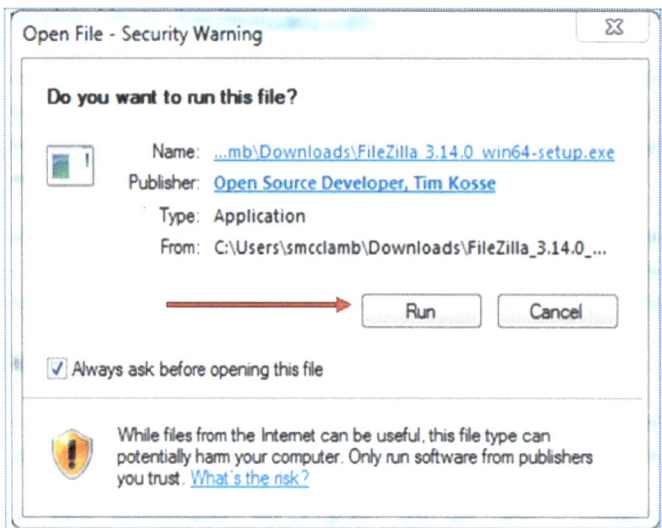

STEP 7.   Click the **Yes** button. You want the FileZilla FTP Client to make the necessary changes to your computer.

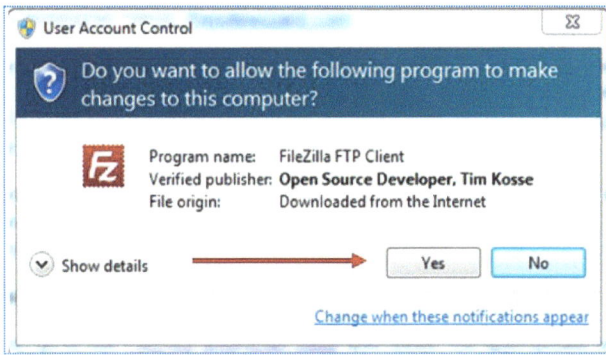

STEP 8.   Click the **I Agree** button to accept the terms of agreement with FileZilla.

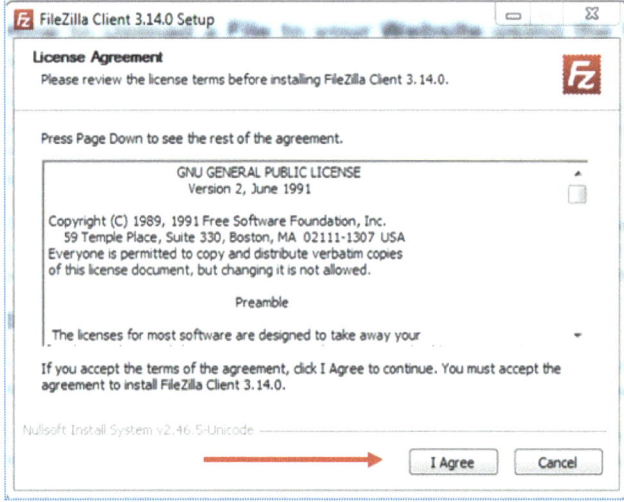

STEP 9.   Select the **Anyone who uses this computer (all users)** option if it is not already selected. Click the **Next** button.

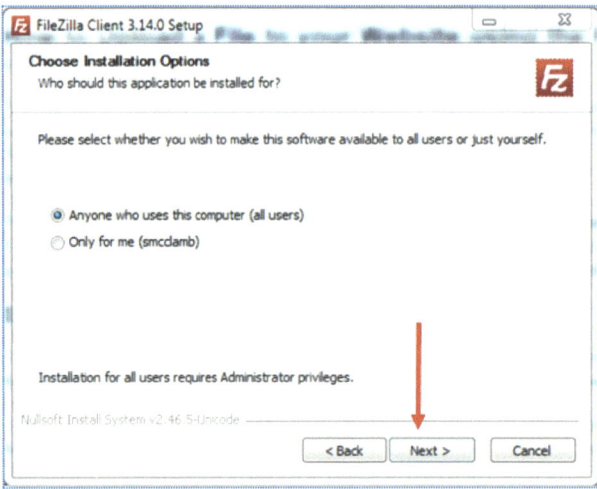

STEP 10.   Place a checkmark in **ALL** of the components to install and click the **Next** button.

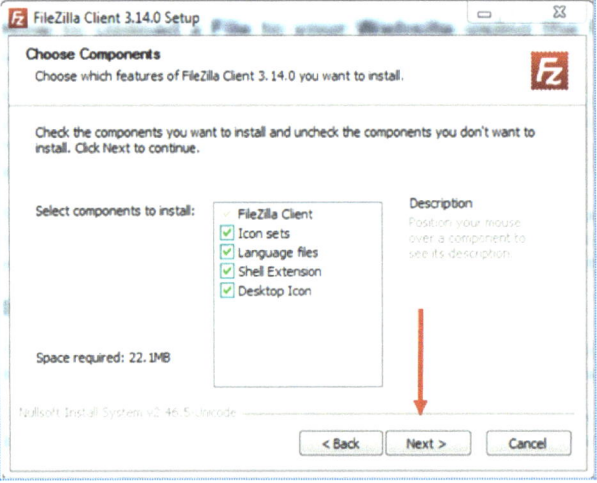

STEP 11.   In most cases, you do not need to change the destination folder. Click the **Next** button.

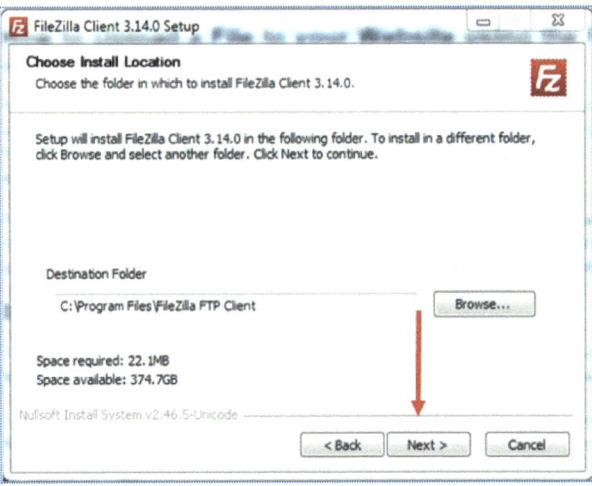

STEP 12.   Use the default **FileZilla FTP Client** folder listed, just click the **Install** button.

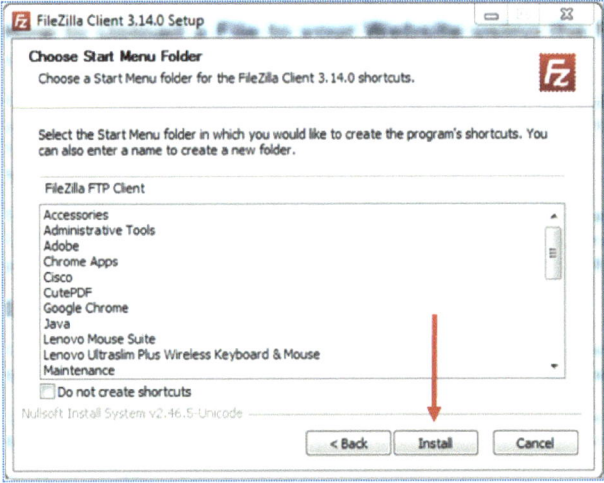

STEP 13.   Click the **Finish** button to complete the install.

Result: The FileZilla FTP Client will open with a message: **Welcome to FileZilla**.

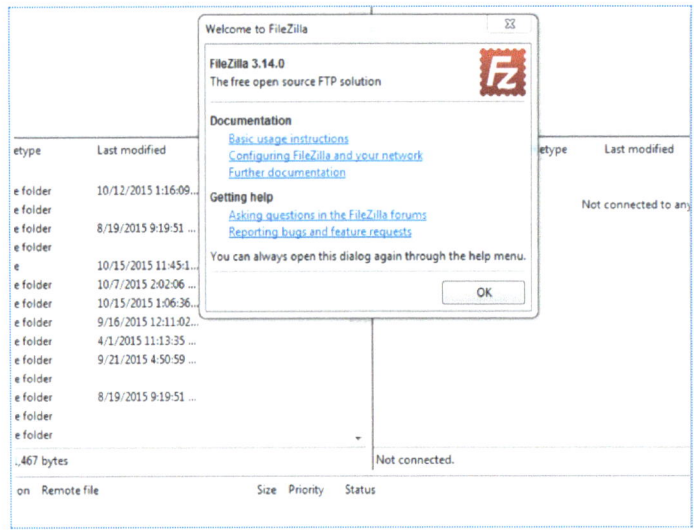

You Have Successfully Downloaded and Opened the FileZilla FTP Client!

Using the FileZilla Quick Connect Bar

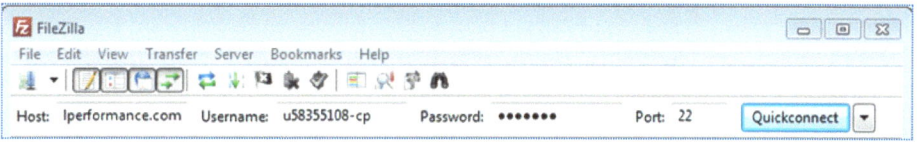

STEP 1.   Fill in the information in the quick connect bar.

Host- This is you domain name or URL	**Port:** The Port for Secure FTP is 22
Username: This is your FTP Username	**Password:** This is your FTP User Password

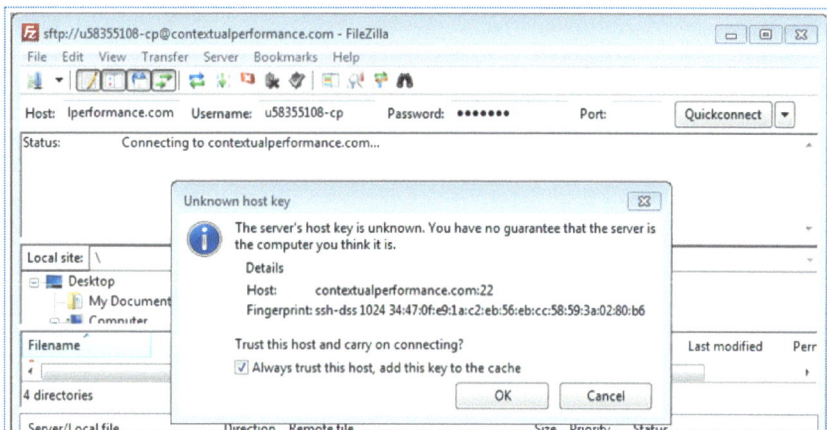

STEP 2. Make sure to check **Always trust this host, add this key to the cache**. Then click the **OK** button.

STEP 3. Click the **Quickconnect** button to connect to the server.

Result: Once established, the connection can be used for uploading or downloading site files.

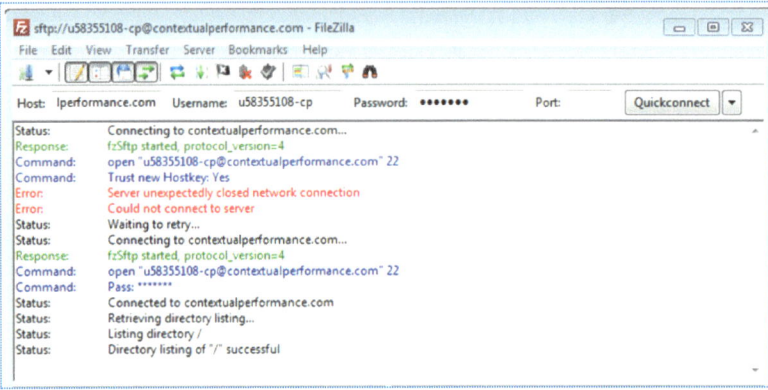

Local and Remote Files in the FTP Client

Local files are located on the left side of the interface and the remote files will be uploaded to the right side.

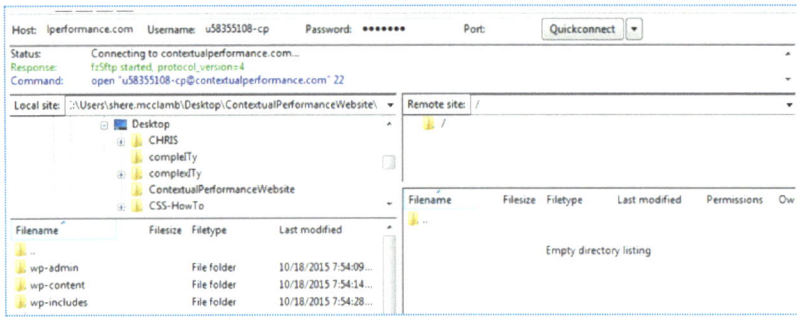

STEP 1. Drag your site **FILES** – not your site **FOLDER** (your local folder name) over to the right side under **Remote site**. You will see the file movement and status updates in the top window. This transfer will take a few second to a minute depending on the amount of data you are transferring.

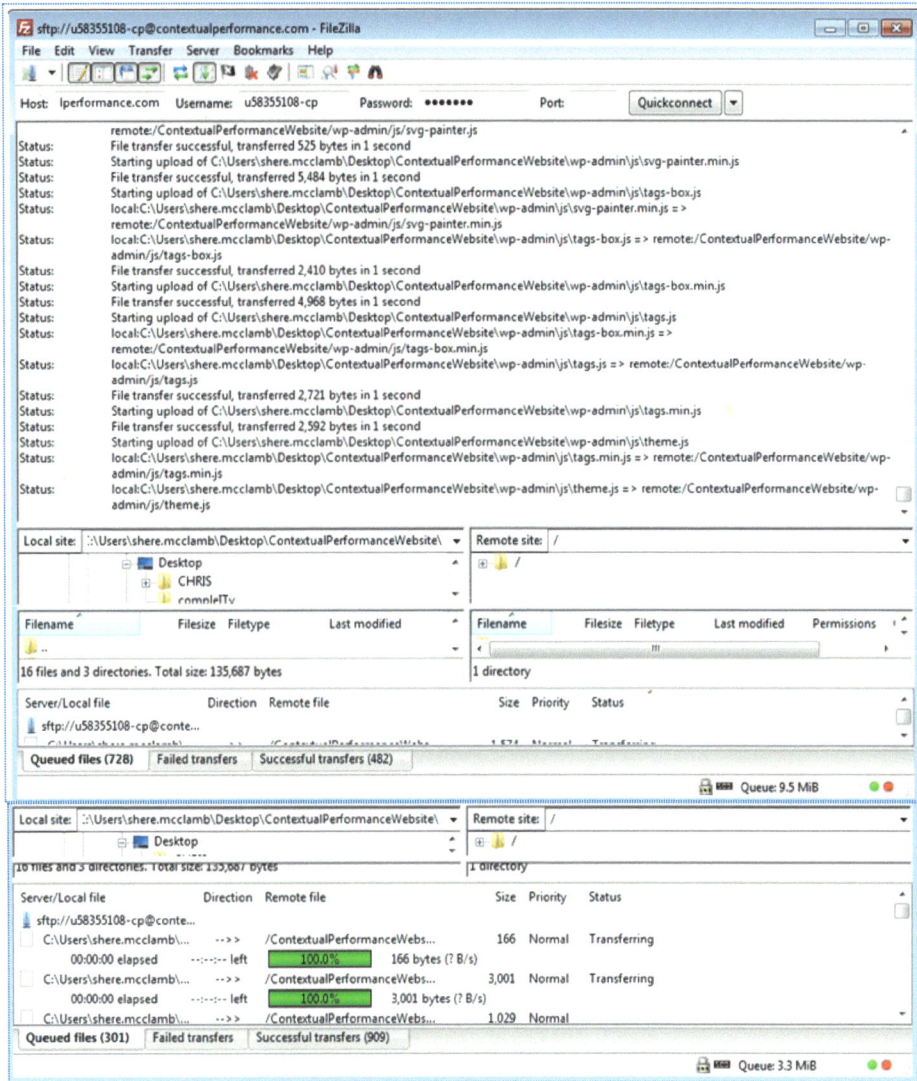

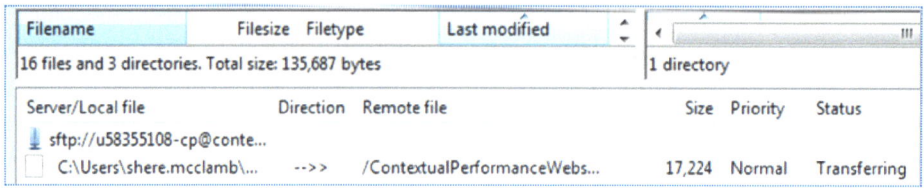

Result: The local files are now on the remote server.

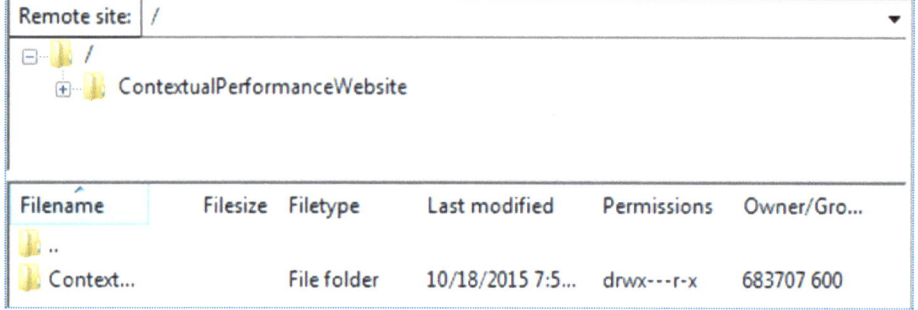

You have successfully transferred the site files to the remote server!

CHAPTER FOUR: THE HTML(5) DOCUMENT

Now that you have some HTML background knowledge under your belt it is time to dive into all of the elements and the order that is required to make up the HTML document.

In this chapter, you will:

- Learn Basic HTML Syntax
- Learn How to use Element Attributes
- Basic HTML Page Structure
- Learn how to use Meta Tags
- Learn how to place Comments in your HTML Code

This chapter introduces you to the basic syntax of HTML tags and the structure of Web pages. There are required layout of elements that all pages require that act as the foundation of the page, provide information to web browsers, the structure of what the users see on the page, and ways for web authors to better organize and document the code.

BASIC HTML SYNTAX

The first step in learning to build web pages is to understand basic structure syntax, meaning how to build web page instructions. The basic building block that displays on the screen is the HTML **tag**. A tag is created using an instruction element called a **character**, surrounded by **brackets**. Everything that you see on a Web page is created by the instructions given to it by the HTML tag.

Tags are created using four keyboard characters:

 **Left-Angle Bracket** – The left-angle bracket is the less-than sign. The less-than sign is created by holding down the shift key and pressing the comma key on the keyboard.

 **Right-Angel Bracket** – The right-angle bracket is the greater-than sign. The greater-than sign is created by holding down the shift key and pressing the period key on the keyboard.

 **Character** – Characters are HTML elements that represent the instructions given to the browser of what to display on the screen that make-up the Web page.

 **Forward Slash** – The forward-slash is a part of the HTML closing tag. The forward-slash is created by pressing the forward-slash key on the keyboard.

The HTML Tag Pair

All of the elements that make up a Web page must be contained within the opening <html> and closing </ html> tags. In other words, all Web page content begin and end with an <html> tag.

The lang (language) attribute is used with the <html> tag to inform the browser which language to expect in the document.

A majority of HTML tags are created using an opening tag and a closing tag that surrounds text that is displayed on screen. The HTML language is created using a set of pre-described tags, some that will be used over and over again, while others will be used more sparingly.

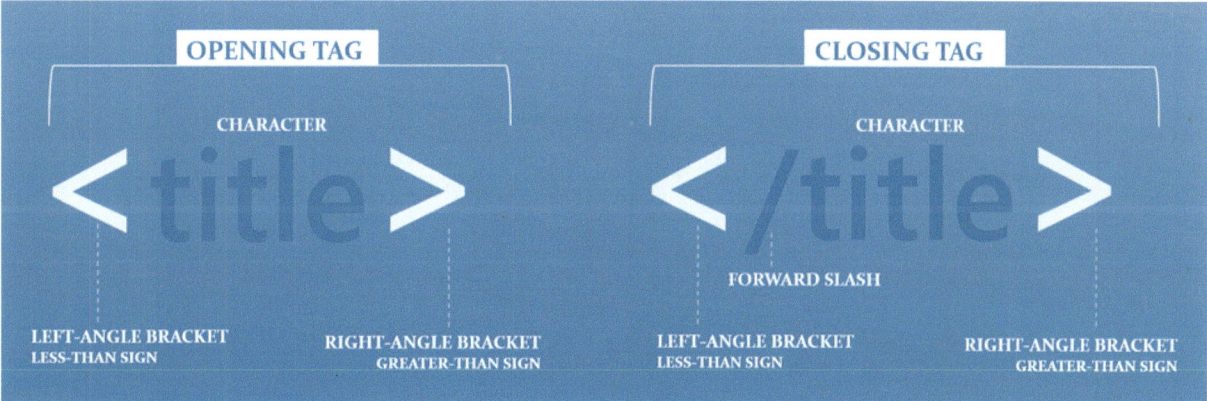

There are also empty elements that do not require a closing tag. They either display a visual element on the page or gives the browser additional instruction, we like to say, they close themselves. HTML5 does not require the closing bracket on empty elements, but I am sure you will see them as you explore the source code of HTML pages.

Line Break	Horizontal Rule	Image
  or 	<hr> or 	<img> or <img/>

There is also a comment tag whose content does not display on the screen, instead it is used to pass on information for those who read the source code of the page. Web author's often use comments to separate the sections of their code and to leave messages to themselves or others about the code they've written.

```
274
275     <!-- is search -->        <div class="content-wrapper">
276     <div class= gdlr-content">
277
278        <!-- Above Sidebar Section-->
279
280        <!-- Sidebar With Content Section-->
281                    <div class="main-content-container container gdlr-item-start-content">
282               <div class="gdlr-item gdlr-main-content">
283                    <div role="form" class="wpcf7" id="wpcf7-f1084-p86-o1" lang="en-US" dir="ltr">
```

ELEMENT ATTRIBUTES

There are some tags require attributes to modify and/or fulfill their ability to give complete directions to the browser to render the HTML document. There is a set of attributes and their accompanying values in the HTML language that are assigned to specific tags. We know that tags are structured using the left (<) and right (>) angle-brackets. To add an attribute to the tag, you will separate it from the tag character with a space (by pressing the space-bar once).

Left-Angle Bracket – Element Character – **Space – Attribute – Equals Sign –** Opening Quotation Mark –

Attribute Property Value – Closing Quotation Mark – **Right-Angle Bracket**

Tags can contain more than one attribute to fulfill the requirements the authors wants for the tag. Attributes are separated by a space.

....attribute="value" attribute="value"....

<link rel="stylesheet" href="style.css"

Attribute Values

The values are attributes, of course, depends on the element you are describing. Values can be words, abbreviations, numbers, or percentages.

Numbers	Alignment	Color	Text
width="#pixels"	align="right"	text="#ff0066"	alt="text"
width="#"	align="center"	border="#3366ff"	target="_blank"

BASIC PAGE STRUCTURE

Pages of a web site range from the most simplistic to extremely complicated, but they all start with the page skeleton that defines the sections of the page, give browsers the instructions it they need to render the pages as intended. There is a basic structure that all web pages must follow. There are tags that are the foundation of all other elements build upon when creating a Web page. Most tags have assigned attributes that further define the actions of the tag. In this text, elements will be displayed in yellow , their attributes in purple , the properties of the attributes in white , and tag characters a document are in blue .

```html
<!DOCTYPE html>
<html lang="en">

    <head>

        <meta charset="utf-8">
        <title>Page Title</title>
        <link rel="stylesheet" href="style.css">

    </head>
    <body>
        <--Page Content Here-->
    </body>

</html>
```

HTML Declarations

All Web pages will start with a DOCTYPE Declaration. It must be the very first item on the page. The purpose of this declaration is to inform the browser prior to any parsing and rendering, what type of document it is working with. Even though DOCTYPE Declaration is not case sensitive it is considered best practice to type the word DOCTYPE in all caps and html in lowercase letters.

<!DOCTYPE html>	<html></html>
HTML5 DOCTYPE Declaration (Required)	Root HTML Element (Required)
	<html lang="en">
	Language Declaration

The HEAD Tag

The elements of the document's head do not render as part of the Web page the users sees. Instead its contents relay information to the browser that affects the rendering of the page.

You will find conflicting information concerning the use of the <head> tag. I recommend applying this a part of your definition of a well-formed document.

Meta Tag

Meta Tags are used to provide key information about your Web page to the browsers that will parse and render them. They are assisted by Meta Attributes that passes the information from the page to the browser.

The Charset Attribute

Unicode Transformation Format (UTF) – Character Encoding (charset) Declaration.

<meta charset="UTF-8">

Character Encoding (character set) Declaration

```
<head>
    <meta charset="UTF-8" />
    <meta name="viewport" content="initial-scale = 1.0" />
    <title>The Bita Group </title>
```

The Name Attribute

The name and content attributes work together to mainly present SEO information about the page. The content usually can be found on the page returned in search engine results.

<meta name="description" content="description">

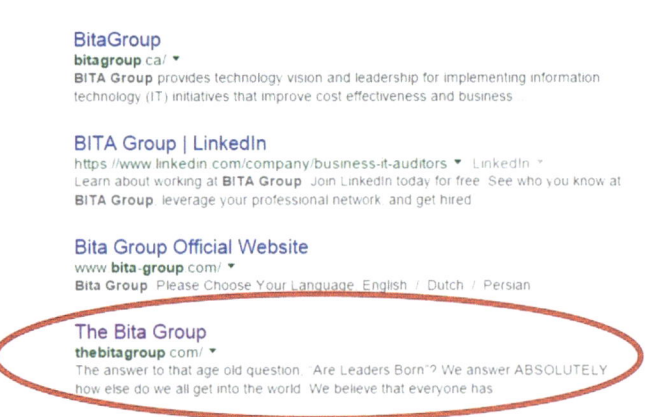

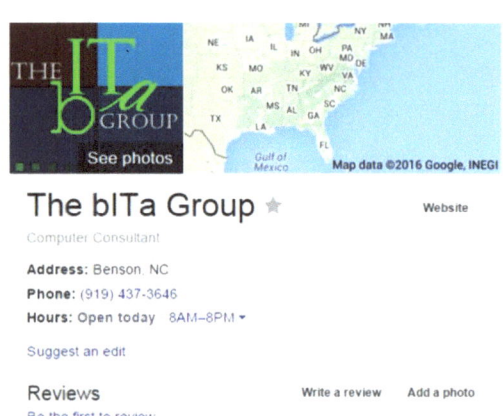

There are many other uses for the name attribute.

<Meta Name="keywords " Contents="words,separwated,by,commas">
Supplies keywords to the search engines when sydering Web sites.

<Meta Name="description" Content="HTML/CSS Basics Class">
A description of the page for search engines that use them on their results pages.

<Meta Name="author" Content="Dr. Shere L.H. McClamb">
Tells search engines who created the pags.

<Meta Name="copyright " Content="Copyright The bITa Group">
Provides Copyright inforation for the page.

The Robot Attribute

<meta name="robots" content="*see chart*"

noindex	Web page will not be indexed.
nofollow	Links on the Web page will not be followed during indexing.
nosnippet	Descriptions of the Web site/Web page will not be provided on search engine result pages.
noodp	Blocks most of the other descriptions from being provided on search engine result pages.
noarchive	Links on the Web page will not be cached for faster loading.
unavailable_after:[date]	The date and time you want robots to stop crawling and indexing the Web page.
noimageindex	Images from your site that appear in search results will not have links that lead back to your pages.
none	is equal to noindex and nofollow

The Title Tag

<title>The Web Page's Title</title>

The contents of the title tag displays on the tab as the document name.

The Link Tag

With the link tag favicons can be specified for Web Sites, Macs, iPhones, and the GNOME (Open Source) Project. Icons are the extra-small images that are in front of the Web Site name in the URL bar.
The **<link rel="prefetch" href="URL">** link tag tells the browser to cache the URL.

<link rel=icon ref="favicon.ico">

<link rel=icon href="favicon.ico">

<link rel=icon href="mac.icns" sizes="128x128 512x512 8192x8192 32768x32768">

<link rel=icon href="iphone.png" sizes="57x57" type="image/png">

<link rel=icon href="gnome.svg" sizes="any" type="image/svg+xml">

```
`http://thebitagroup.com/wp-content/plugins/masterslider/public/assets/css/common/grab.cur`;
</script>
<link rel="shortcut icon" href="http://thebitagroup.com/wp-content/uploads/2015/10/favicon-
32x32.png" type="image/x-icon" /><!-- load the script for older ie version -->
<!-- [if lt IE 9]>
<script src="http://thebitagroup.com/wp-content/themes/clevercourse-v1-
```

The <link> Attributes

rel="alternate"

```
<link rel="alternate" type="application/rss+xml" title="The Bita Group &raquo; Feed" href="http://thebitagroup.com/feed/" />
<link rel="alternate" type="application/rss+xml" title="The Bita Group &raquo; Comments Feed" href="http://thebitagroup.com/comments/feed/" />
<link rel="alternate" type="text/calendar" title="The Bita Group &raquo; iCal Feed" href="http://thebitagroup.com/events/?ical=1" />
```

rel="stylesheet"

```
35  <link rel='stylesheet' id='opinionstage-style-css' href='http://thebitagroup.com/wp-
    content/plugins/social-polls-by-opinionstage/opinionstage-style-common.css?ver=4.4.2'
    type='text/css' media='all' />
36  <link rel='stylesheet' id='opinionstage-font-style-css' href='http://thebitagroup.com/wp-
    content/plugins/social-polls-by-opinionstage/opinionstage-font.css?ver=4.4.2' type='text/css'
    media='all' />
37  <link rel='stylesheet' id='bbp-default-css' href='http://thebitagroup.com/wp-
    content/plugins/bbpress/templates/default/css/bbpress.css?ver=2.5.8-5815' type='text/css'
    media='screen' />
```

The Body Tag

Everything you want the user to see will reside between the opening and closing <body> tags.

<body>Content of the Web page</body>

opening <body> tag

```
126     ***2301,Opacity. 1,j]></style></head>
127     <body class="home page-template-default page page-id-42 _masterslider _msp_version_3.0.4 tribe-no-js">
128     <img class="gdlr-full-boxed-background" src="http://fmbcsmithfield.org/wp-content/uploads/2018/04/red-
        orange-soft-carpet-texture-background.jpg" alt="" /><div class="body-wrapper gdlr-boxed-style" data-
        home="http://fmbcsmithfield.org" >
129             <header class="gdlr-header-wrapper">
130             <!-- top navigation -->
131                 <div class="top-navigation-wrapper">
132                 <div class="top-navigation-container container">
```

EVERYTHING DISPLAYED ON THE SCREEN IS HERE

```
459     /* <![CDATA[ */
460     var a3_lazyload_extend_params = {"edgeY":"0"};
461     /* ]]> */
462     </script>
463     <script type='text/javascript' src='//fmbcsmithfield.org/wp-content/plugins/a3-lazy-
        load/assets/js/jquery.lazyloadxt.extend.js?ver=1.9.2'></script>
464     <script type='text/javascript' src='http://fmbcsmithfield.org/wp-includes/js/wp-embed.min.js?ver=5.1.1'>
        </script>
465     </body>
466     </html>
```

closing <body> tag

CHAPTER FIVE: THE DOCUMENT STRUCTURE

> *Now that you have a grasp of the basic structure of the HTML document, let's build on that by creating the body section of the page using 7 content model categories and their attributes.*

In this chapter, you will:

- Learn HTML5's 7 Content Model Categories
- Learn the Global and Main Attributes Shape HTML Elements
- Learn the how to properly Outline HTML Page Content
- Learn how to structure Self-Closing Tags
- Learn How to Code Special Characters

Mapping out you document prior to coding it in HTML can go a long way in helping you see the tags you need to outline your content. Using the HTML content algorithm brings how to accomplish this into focus. Even though many of the pages on the Internet have not been written in HTML, you will gain insightful knowledge on outlining that will help to break through the confusing when writing your own code.

STRUCTURAL ELEMENTS

There are a number of new elements for the newest version of HTML5. Many of them give specific names to structural elements of the web page. Using these new elements will increase the usability and maintainability of your code. The elements are easy to remember in a large part because they describe what to expect in each part of the page. For those who are new to the language, I am sure you will wonder, what did you use before?

The 7 content model categories in HTML5:

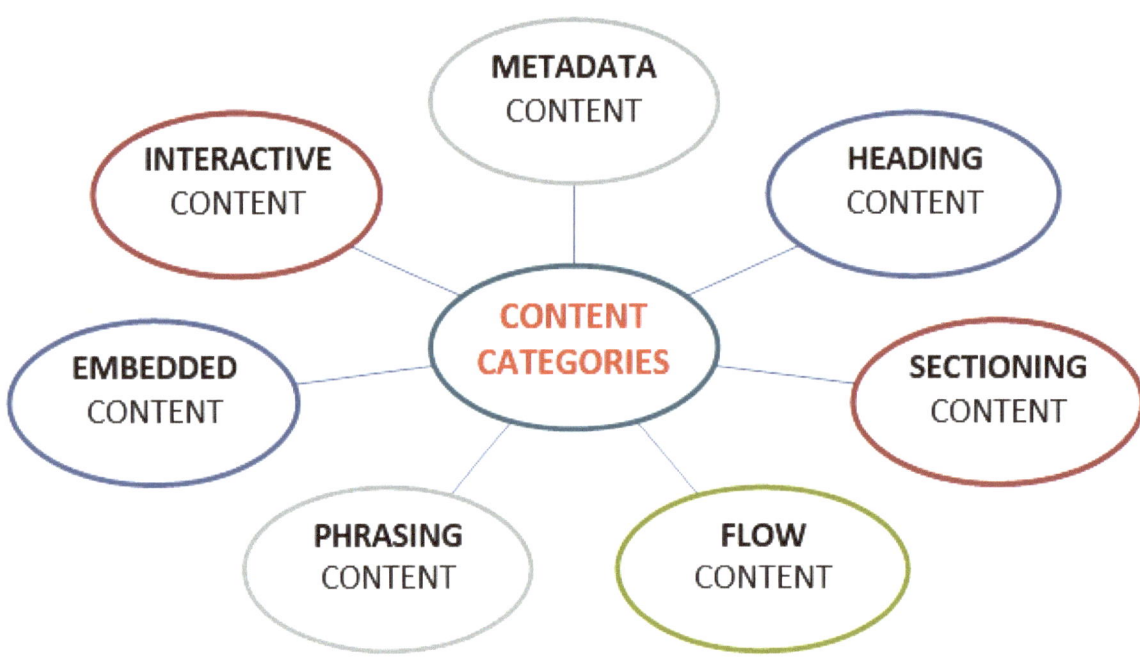

Metadata content is found in the <head> of an HTML document. These tags and attributes set up how the browser presents the page data on the screens and interprets of behavioral of the document. The elements for the metadata content are:

<link>

<link rel="stylesheet" href= "location and file name" type="text/css">

The link tag informs the browser that there is a sheet of styles in another location it should parse to format the Web page.

> **link rel= "stylesheet" href= "css file location/name.css" type="text/css"**

<base>

> **<base href="web_address" target="_blank">**

The base tag set the URL default address for the site. In other words, all of the pages accessed from this website will start with this Web address.

<command>

<meta http-equiv="refresh" content="n">

The http-equiv commands the Web browser to perform the action of "refreshing" action. In this case it is to refresh the page in "n" number of seconds. Accessibility standards discourages using the system to perform unrequested actions.

<meta http-equiv="refresh" content="number of seconds">

<meta>

<Meta Name="generator" Content="WordPres x.x.x">.

This generator attribute tells search engines which program createf the web page. In this case it was a version of WordPress.

<meta name="Generator" content="WordPressx.x.x">

```
81  <meta name="generator" content="WordPress 4.4.2" />
82  <meta name="generator" content="WooCommerce 2.5.2" />
```

<noscript>

<noscript>Your Browser Does Not Support JavaScript</noscript>.

This statement let's the person accessing a site that uses JavaScript that it is either turned off or their browsers does not support it.

<noscript>Your Browser Does Not Support JavaScript</noscript>

<script>

> **<script type="javascript"> JavaScript Code Here</script>**

The script tag encloses scripting within the head of the document. The type attribute describes the kind of script presented between the opening and closing script tags.

```
<script type="text/javascript" >
window._wpemojiSettings =
{"baseUrl":"https:\/\/s.w.org\/images\/core\/emoji\/72x72\/","ext":".png","source":{"concatemoji":"http:\/\/thebitagroup.com\/wp-includes\/js\/wp-
emoji-release.min.js?ver=4.4.2"}};
!function(a,b,c){function d(a){var c,d=b.createElement("canvas"),e=d.getContext&&d.getContext("2d"),f=String.fromCharCode;return
e&&e.fillText?(e.textBaseline="top",e.font="600 32px
Arial","flag"===a?(e.fillText(f(55356,56806,55356,56826),0,0),d.toDataURL().length>3e3):"diversity"===a?(e.fillText(f(55356,57221),0,0),c=e.getImageData(16,16,
1,1).data.toString(),e.fillText(f(55356,57221,55356,57343),0,0),c!==e.getImageData(16,16,1,1).data.toString()):("simple"===a?e.fillText(f(55357,56835),0,0):e.fillT
ext(f(55356,57135),0,0),0!==e.getImageData(16,16,1,1).data[0])):!1}function e(a){var
c=b.createElement("script");c.src=a,c.type="text/javascript",b.getElementsByTagName("head")[0].appendChild(c)}var
f,g;c.supports={simple:d("simple"),flag:d("flag"),unicode8:d("unicode8"),diversity:d("diversity")},c.DOMReady=!1,c.readyCallback=function(){c.DOMReady=!
0},c.supports.simple&&c.supports.flag&&c.supports.unicode8&&c.supports.diversity||(g=function(){c.readyCallback()},b.addEventListener?(b.addEventList
ener("DOMContentLoaded",g,!1),a.addEventListener("load",g,!1)):(a.attachEvent("onload",g),b.attachEvent("onreadystatechange",function(){"complete"=
==b.readyState&&c.readyCallback()})),f=c.source||{},f.concatemoji?e(f.concatemoji):f.wpemoji&&f.twemoji&&(e(f.twemoji),e(f.wpemoji)))}(window,doc
ument,window._wpemojiSettings);
</script>
```

<title>

<title> JavaScript Code Here</title>

The title tag encloses the title or name of the Web between the opening and closing title tag in the head of the document.

> **<title>The Web Page's Title</title>**

<style>

<style type="text/css"> Style Declarations Here</style>

The style tag encloses stle declarations within the head of the document. The type attribute describes this to be text used to create cascading stylesheet declarations will be presented between the opening and closing style tags.

```
<style type="text/css">
img.wp-smiley,
img.emoji {
        display: inline !important;
        border: none !important;
        box-shadow: none !important;
        height: 1em !important;
        width: 1em !important;
        margin: 0 .07em !important;
        vertical-align: -0.1em !important;
        background: none !important;
        padding: 0 !important;
        }
</style>
```

HEADING AND SECTION CATEGORIES

Heading Category

<header > *(New in 5)*
Represents a group of introductory or navigational aids. The header tag can be placed several times within the same document.

START PAGE HEADING	<header>
	<h1>The Title Text</h1>
END PAGE HEADING	</header>

Header Heading Levels

<h1>Largest Heading Level</h1>
<h2>Smaller</h2>
<h3>Smaller</h3>
<h4>Smaller</h4>
<h5>Smaller</h5>
<h6>Smallest Heading Level</h6>

<Hgroup> *(New in 5)*
Represents the header of a section.

START HEADING GROUP	<Hgroup>
	<h1>Main Title</h1>
	<h2>Subtitle</h2>
	<h1>Author</h1>
END HEADING GROUP	</Hgroup>

Sectioning Category

<section> *(New in 5)*

Represents a generic document or application section. It can be used together with the h1, h2, h3, h4, h5, and h6 elements to indicate the document structure.

START PAGE SECTION	**<section>**
	<p>Content</p>
	<p>Content</p>
END PAGE SECTION	**</section>**

<article> *(New in 5)*

represents an independent piece of content of a document, such as a blog entry or newspaper article.

START ARTICLE	**<article>**
	<h2>Article Heading</h2>
	<p>Article Content</p>
END ARTICLE	**</article>**

<nav> *(New in 5)*

represents a section of the document intended for navigation.

START NAVIGATION (Unordered List)	**<ul>**
	<li> <a href="#">Home</a> </li>
	<li> <a href="#">Courses</a> </li>
	<li> <a href="#">Sign Up</a> </li>
END NAVIGATION	**</ul>**

<div>

Defines a division or a section that is often used as a container for other HTML elements to style them with CSS.

START DIVISION	**<div>**
	<h3>Article Heading</h3>
	<p>Article Content</p>
END DIVISION	**</div>**

<footer> *(New in 5)*

Represents a footer for a section that contains information about the author, copyright information, etc.

START PAGE FOOTER	**<ul>**
	<p>&copy; - All Rights Reserved </p>
END PAGE FOOTER	**</ul>**

THE OTHER 5 HTML5 CONTENT CATEGORIES

The content categories of flow, phrasing, embedded, and interactive will all be contained within the opening <body> and closing </body> tags. You will find that there will be a subset of elements that you will use with regularity while others are used sparingly or on occasion. Once the routinely used elements are committed to memory you will be on your way to creating web pages with ease.

Elements will overlap categories, Don't be surprised if you see tags being used in more than one situation as you create your Web pages. Remember it's about content not display.

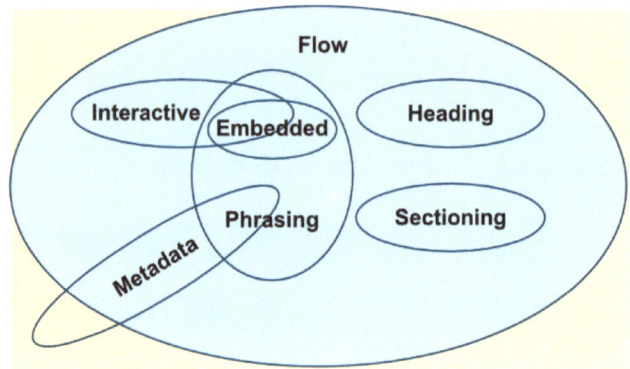

Flow Content

> Content that is primarily text or embedded.

Phrasing Content

> Content that contains phrasing content make up the paragraphs of the Web page.

Embedded Content

> Content that imports other resources (audio, video, etc.) into the document.

Interactive Content

> Content specifically intended for interaction with the user.

Elements of the Flow, Phrasing, Embedded, and Interactive Categories

ELEMENTS	ATTRIBUTES	CATEGORIES
a	href target rel media hreflang type	Flow
abbr	title	Flow and Phrasing
address	GLOABAL ATTRIBUTES ONLY	Flow
area	EMPTY	Flow and Phrasing
	alt coords shape href target rel media hreflang type	Flow and Phrasing
article	GLOABAL ATTRIBUTES ONLY	Flow and Sectioning
aside	GLOABAL ATTRIBUTES ONLY	Flow and Sectioning
audio	src preload autoplay mediagroup loop muted controls	Flow, Phrasing, and Embedded
b	GLOBAL ATTRIBUTES ONLY	Flow and Phrasing
bdi	dir	Flow and Phrasing
bdo	dir	Flow and Sectioning
blockquote	cite	Flow and Sectioning
br	GLOBAL ATTRIBUTES ONLY	Flow and Phrasing
button	autofocus disabled	Flow, Phrasing, and Interactive

	form formaction formenctype formmethod formnovalidate formtarget name type value	
canvas	width height	Flow, Phrasing, and Embedded
cite	GLOBAL ATTRIBUTES ONLY	Flow and Phrasing
code	GLOBAL ATTRIBUTES ONLY	GLOBAL ATTRIBUTES
command	type label icon disabled checked radiogroup	Metadata, Flow, and Phrasing
datalist	The datalist element is hooked up to an input element using the list attribute on the input element.	Flow and Phrasing
del	cite datetime	Flow
details	open	Flow, Sectioning, and Interactive
dfn	title	Flow and Phrasing
div	GLOBAL ATTRIBUTES ONLY	Flow
dl	GLOBAL ATTRIBUTES ONLY	Flow

em	GLOBAL ATTRIBUTES ONLY	Flow and Phrasing
embed	src type width height	Flow, Sectioning, Embedded, and Interactive
fieldset	disabled form name	Flow and Sectioning
figure	GLOBAL ATTRIBUTES ONLY	Flow and Sectioning
footer	GLOBAL ATTRIBUTES ONLY	
form	GLOBAL ATTRIBUTES ONLY	Flow
h1	GLOBAL ATTRIBUTES ONLY	Flow and Heading
h2	GLOBAL ATTRIBUTES ONLY	Flow and Heading
h3	GLOBAL ATTRIBUTES ONLY	Flow and Heading
h4	GLOBAL ATTRIBUTES ONLY	Flow and Heading
h5	GLOBAL ATTRIBUTES ONLY	Flow and Heading
h6	GLOBAL ATTRIBUTES ONLY	Flow and Heading
header	GLOBAL ATTRIBUTES ONLY	Flow and Heading
hgroup	GLOBAL ATTRIBUTES ONLY	Flow and Heading
hr	EMPTY ELEMENT	Flow
i	GLOBAL ATTRIBUTES ONLY	Flow and Phrasing
iframe	src srcdoc name sandbox seamless width height	Flow, Phrasing, Embedded, and Interactive
img	alt src usemap ismap width height	Flow, Phrasing, Embedded, and Interactive
input	accept alt	Flow, Phrasing, and Interactive

	autocomplete autofocus checked dirname disabled form formaction formenctype formmethod formnovalidate formtarget height list max maxlength min multiple name pattern placeholder readonly required size src step type value width	
ins	GLOBAL ATTRIBUTES ONLY	Flow
kbd	GLOBAL ATTRIBUTES ONLY	Flow and Phrasing
keygen	autofocus challenge disabled form keytype name	Flow, Phrasing, and Interactive

label	form	Flow, Phrasing, and Interactive

map	name	Flow
mark	GLOBAL ATTRIBUTES ONLY	Flow and Phrasing
menu	type label	Flow
meter	value min max low high optimum form	Flow and Phrasing

nav	GLOBAL ATTRIBUTES ONLY	Flow and Sectioning
noscript	GLOBAL ATTRIBUTES ONLY	Metadata, Flow and Phrasing

object	data type name usemap form width height	Flow, Phrasing, Embedded, and Interactive
ol	reversed start type	Flow
output	for form name	Flow and Phrasing

p	GLOBAL ATTRIBUTES ONLY	Flow
pre	GLOBAL ATTRIBUTES ONLY	Flow
progress	GLOBAL ATTRIBUTES ONLY	Flow and Phrasing

q	cite	Flow and Phrasing

ruby	GLOBAL ATTRIBUTES ONLY	Flow and Phrasing

s	GLOBAL ATTRIBUTES ONLY	Flow and Phrasing
samp	GLOBAL ATTRIBUTES ONLY	Flow and Phrasing
script	src	Metadata, Flow and Phrasing

	async defer type charset	
section	GLOBAL ATTRIBUTES ONLY	Flow and Sectioning
select	autofocus disabled form multiple name required size	Flow, Phrasing, and Interactive
small	GLOBAL ATTRIBUTES ONLY	Flow and Phrasing
span	GLOBAL ATTRIBUTES ONLY	Flow and Phrasing
strong	GLOBAL ATTRIBUTES ONLY	Flow and Phrasing
style	media type scoped title	Metadata and Flow
sub	GLOBAL ATTRIBUTES ONLY	Flow and Phrasing
sup	GLOBAL ATTRIBUTES	Flow and Phrasing
svg		

table	border	Flow
textarea	autofocus cols dirname disabled form maxlength name placeholder readonly required rows wrap	Flow, Phrasing, and Interactive
time	datetime pubdate	Flow and Phrasing
u	GLOBAL ATTRIBUTES ONLY	Flow and Phrasing
ul	GLOBAL ATTRIBUTES ONLY	Flow
var	GLOBAL ATTRIBUTES ONLY	Flow and Phrasing

video	src poster preload autoplay mediagroup loop muted controls width height	Flow, Embedded, and Phrasing
wbr	EMPTY ELEMENT	Flow and Phrasing

Global and Key HTML5 Element Attributes

Global Attributes – All Elements Use Global Attributes	
accesskey	A guide when creating a keyboard shortcut to activate or focus an element.
contenteditable	An enumerated [empty] attribute whose keywords are: true and false.
contextmenu	The content of an element's context menu when requested by right-clicking the element, or pressing a context menu key.
draggable	An enumerated attribute with three states. 1st = True 2nd = False 3rd= auto.
dir	Specifies text directionality (e.g. left-to-right (ltr) and right-to-left (rtl).
dropzone	The value of the area where an element will land when dragged.
lang	Specifies the primary language of the document.
hidden	Indicates the relevance of an element is: not yet or no longer relevant.
id	An element's unique identifier (ID).
spellcheck	An enumerated attribute whose keywords are: empty, string, true, and false.
style	A Cascading Style Sheet attribute.
tabindex	Specifies whether the element is focusable.
title	Advisory information for an element,(e.g. the title of a page or a tooltip).

Key Attributes	
src	Supplies the address of a page.
href	Supplies the target URL.
media	Describes target URL or style.
hreflang	Specifies the language of a linked resource.
preload	Specifies which elements should be loaded prior to the document.
type	Controls the behavior of a button when depressed.
label	Supplies the name of the command that is visible to the user.
icon	Supplies a picture that represents the command.
name	Allows for the use of specific description information.
cite	Specifies a title (e.g. a book, movie, video, etc.).
seamless	Content contained within an iframe should render seamlessly on the screen.
reversed	Indicates that the lists can be presented as: descending (3, 2, and 1).
charset	Specifies the character encoding of as external script resource.

OUTLINING ALGORITHM MODEL

Understanding the Outlining Algorithm/Structure

In HTML5, each part of the Web page is contained within its own section. The distinction is made because the majority of the Web pages found on the Internet today is creating by coding that do not follow HTML5 markup recommendations. The first heading <h1> thru <h6> defines the heading of that section.

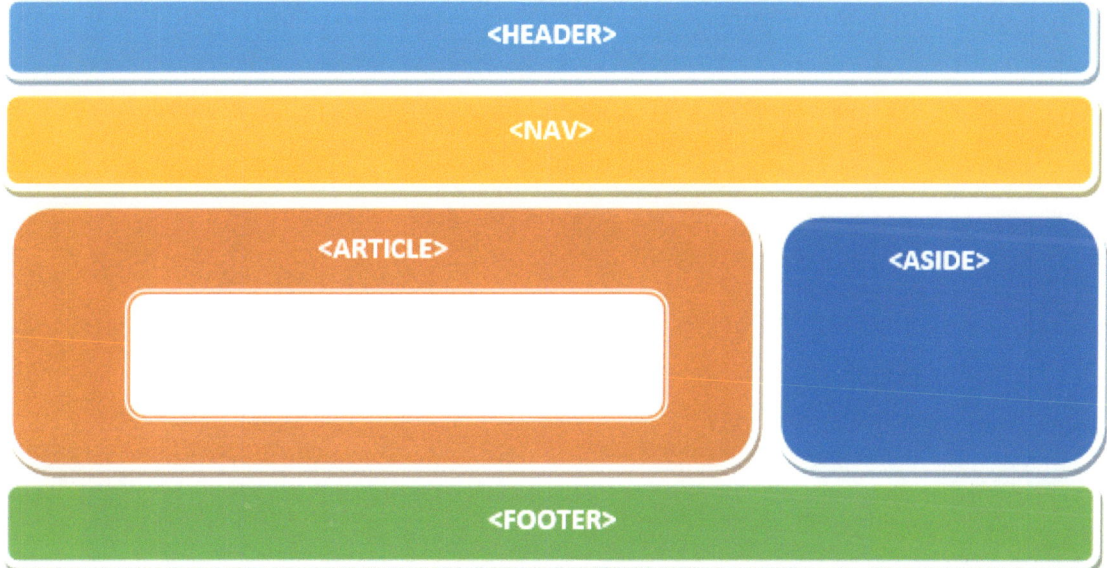

Building a Section of a Web Page

	Open the body of the HTML document	`<body>`
1.	Create a Section	`<section>`
	Create the heading of the section	`<h1> Heading for section 1</h1>`
	Create the content for the section	`<p>Content for section1</p>`
	Close the section	`</section>`
	Close the body of the HTML document	`</body`

Building Multiple Sections of a Web Page

		Open the body of the HTML document	`<body>`
1.		**Create Section 1**	`<section>`
	1.1	Create the 1ST section in section 1	`<section>`
		Create the 1ST heading in section 1	`<h1> 1st Heading in section 1</h1>`
		Create the content for the section 1	`<p>Content for section1</p>`
		Close the 1ST section in section 1	`</section>`
	1.2	Create the 2nd section in section 1	`<section>`
		Create the 2nd heading in section 1	`<h1> 1st Heading in section 1</h1>`
		Create the content for the section 1	`<p>Content for section1</p>`
		Close the 2nd section in section 1	`</section>`
		Close section 1	`</section>`
		Close the body of the HTML document	`</body`

96

SELF-CLOSING TAGS

Tags that do not contain data are called empty tags. In HTML5, they do not require a forward slash (/) at the end of the tag as in previous versions of HTML. Both style of writing the tags is included in the chart because you will undoubtedly encounter both versions when reading code from older versions.

Horizontal Rule Tag

<hr />
<hr>

`<hr>`

An element used to separate Web page content. In HTML5 is referred to as a thematic break.

Line Break Tag

`<br>`

An element used enter a single break in a line. Its operation is similar to holding down shift and pressing enter to go to the next line in text editors.

Image Tag

<img src="#" />
<img src="#">

`<img>`

An element used to place an image in the page. There are several attributes to enhance and make images more accessible.
Required Attributes: src | alt
Not Required: width | height | style

Comment Tag

`<!--Comment goes here.-->`

The content of a comment does not display on the screen, instead it is used to pass on information for those who read the source code of the page. Web author's often use comments to separate the sections of their code and to leave messages to themselves or others about the code they've written.

SPECIAL CHARACTERS

In HTML, keyboard representations for symbols are not allowable. Special characters are created using a combination of the ampersand (&) numbers and/or characters and the semi-colon (;). There are literally hundreds to choose from. Special characters are easy to find on the Web. Just type HTML Special Characters into any search engine.

CHARACTER	REPRESENTS	NUMBER	ENTITY
BUSINESS			
©	COPYRIGHT SYMBOL	&#169;	&copy;
®	REGISTRATION SYBOL	&#174;	&reg;
™	TRADEMARK SYBOL	&#8482;	&trade;
ARROWS			
←	LEFT ARROW	&#8592;	&larr;
→	RIGHT ARROW	&#8594;	&rarr;
↑	UP ARROW	&#8593;	&uarr;
↓	DOWN ARROW	&#8595;	&darr;
STARS			
★	BLACK STAR	&#2605;	
☆	WHITE STAR	&#2606	
PHONES			
☎	BLACK PHONE	&#260E	
☏	WHITE PHONE	&#260F;	
SELECTION			
☐	EMPTY BOX	&#2610;	
☑	CHECKED BOX	&#2611;	
☒	X'ED BOX	&#2612;	
SIGNS			
♻	RECYCLING SIGN BLACK	&#267B;	
♿	WHEELCHAIR SIGN	&#267F;	
⚡	VOLTAGE SIGN	&#26A1;	

UTF_8 Geometric Shapes – Ranging from Hexadecimal - &#25A0; to &#25FF;

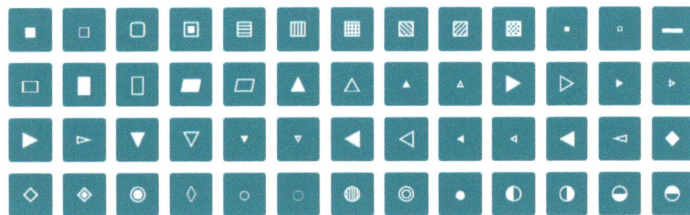

UTF_8 Block Elements – Ranging from Hexadecimal - ਔ to &#259f;

UTF_8 Miscellaneous Symbols – Ranging from Hexadecimal - ਨ to &#26FF;

UTF_8 Dingbats – Ranging from Hexadecimal - ઌ to &#27BF;

CHAPTER SIX: LISTS, LINKS, AND IMAGES

The ability to create lists is a staple of any document; linking pages and Web sites is the basis of the Internet; and of course, the Web would be a visual boring space without images. Chapter 5 covers them all!

In this chapter, you will:

- Learn how to create ordered (numbered), unordered (bulleted), and definition lists
- Learn to create hyperlinks
- Insert images into the page and make them links

In this chapter, you will learn the fundamentals of creating from the simplest to more complex list using the <ol> ordered and <ul> list tags. You will to create internal and external text, image and document links.

LISTS

Lists have been a staple of Web sites since the beginning of the Web. Learning how to create and control the nesting of list is an important tool for your HTML toolbox.

Ordered Lists

Ordered list, known as numbered lists are created using the:

An opening and closing <ol> Ordered List Tag to create the list and an opening and closing <li> List Item Tag for each item in the list.

Open an ordered list.	**<ul>**
Open/Close the 1st numbered list item.	<li></li>
Open/Close the 2nd numbered list item.	<li></li>
Open/Close the 3rd numbered list item.	<li></li>
Close the ordered list.	**</ul>**

Unordered Lists

Unordered list, known as bulleted lists are created using the:

An opening and closing <ul> Unordered List Tag to create the list and an opening and closing <li> List Item Tag for each item in the list.

Open an unordered list.	**<ul>**
Open/Close the 1st bulleted list item.	<li></li>
Open/Close the 2nd bulleted list item.	<li></li>
Open/Close the 3rd bulleted list item.	<li></li>
Close the unordered list.	**</ul>**

Definition Lists

Definition list is used to create a glossary-like list using the:

An opening and closing Definition List Tag <dl> to create the list and an opening and closing Definition Term Tag <dt> for the term and Definition's Definition for you guessed it - the definition.

Open a definition list.	<dl>
Open/Close a definition term.	<dt></dt>
Open/Close the definition description.	<dd> </dd>
Open/Close a definition term.	<dt> </dt>
Open/Close the definition description.	<dd> </dd>
Close the definition list.	</dl>

Nested Bulleted List

A mixed list is created using nested bulleted lists used to create a sub-list using the:

Open an unordered list.	<ul>
Open/Close the 1st bulleted list item.	<li> </li>
Open the 2nd bulleted list item.	<li>vvv
Open a bulleted sub-list.	<ul>
Open/Close the 1st bullet in sub-list.	<li> </li>
Open/Close the 2nd bullet in sub-list.	<li> </li>
Close the bulleted list.	</ul>
Close the 2nd bulleted list item.	</li>
Open/Close the 3rd bulleted list item.	<li> </li>
Close the unordered list.	</ul>

Complex Lists

A mixed list is created by nesting an unordered list and an ordered list tags to create complex list:

Open an ordered list.	**<ol>**
Open/Close the 1st numbered list item.	<li> </li>
Open/Close the 2nd numbered list item that has 2 bullets.	<li></li>
Open a bulleted sub-list.	**<ul>**
Open/Close the 1st bullet in sub-list.	<li> </li>
Open/Close the 2nd bullet in sub-list.	<li> </li>
Close the bulleted sub-list.	**</ul>**
End (close) 2nd numbered list item.	</li>
Open/Close the 3rd numbered list item.	<li> </li>
End (close) an ordered list.	**</ol>**

LINKS AND ANCHORS

Text Links

The most basic link to create in HTML is the text link. Placing an anchor <a> tag around text word or words turns them into a hyperlink that takes the user to a destination that resides in the same page or document, to another page or document within the same site, or to another URL completely.

Links are created using the anchor tag <a>. Even though the anchor tag is in some opinion are the bridges that connects the world-wide-Web, it requires the hypertext reference (href) attribute to make any of the magic happen. To create a link there are a few attributes that are required and some that are merely helpers in the linking process.

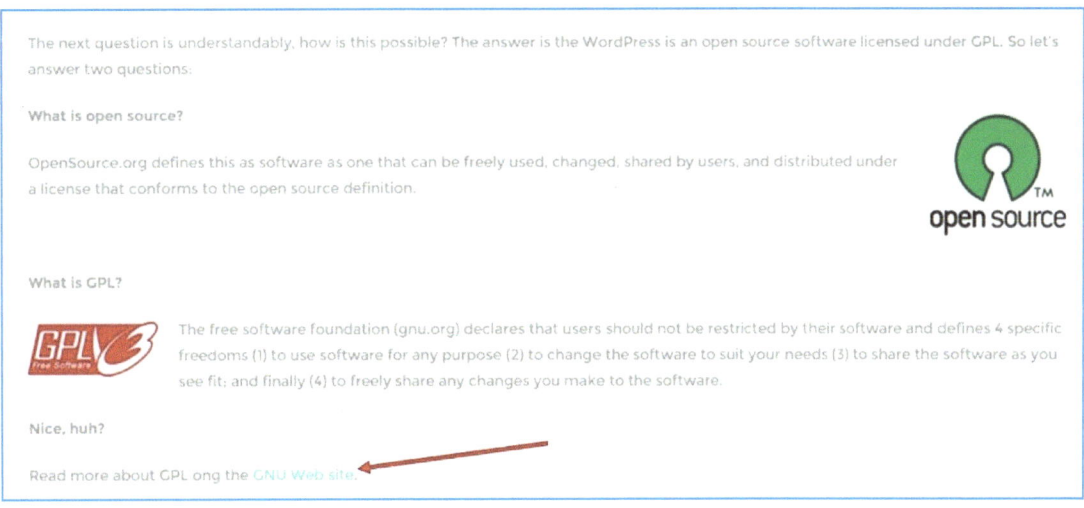

Anchor Tag	Creates a Link	`<a> </a>`
Hypertext Reference Attribute	Link URL	`href="URL"`
Link Text	Link Name the User Sees	text
Target Attribute	Where the destination of the Link will appear.	_blank _self _parent _top

Creating the destination URL

The destination of links are categorized as follows:

Bookmarks – Links that take the user to another area of the same document.

Internal Link – Links that take the user to another page or document in the same Web site.

External Links – Links that take the user to a Web site or document outside of the Web site they were on when they clicked the link.

A basic external text link: **<a href= "http://anotherwebsite.com">Another Web Site</a>**

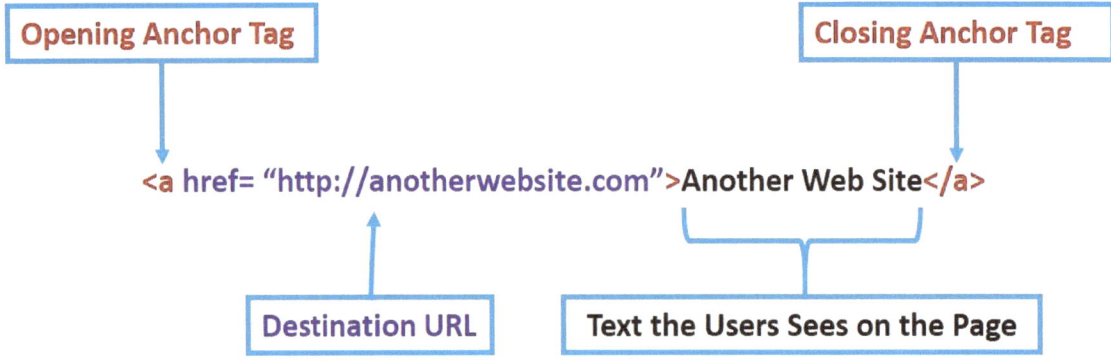

Directing the Target Attribute

When creating a link, the destination (where the user will end up) is controlled by the target attribute. This attribute is not required. When the target attribute is omitted, the new web content, replaces the old content by default. When you have specific destinations for linked content, here are the choices:

Destination Attribute	Attribute in the Link	Destination
_blank	target="_blank"	A new window or tab
_self	target="_self"	*Same window or tab as it was clicked
_parent	target="_parent"	In the parent frame (frames)
_top	target="_top"	The full body of the window (frames)

Putting It All Together to Create a Link

<a href="thebitagroup.com/courses.asp" target="_blank"> Courses I Teach</a>

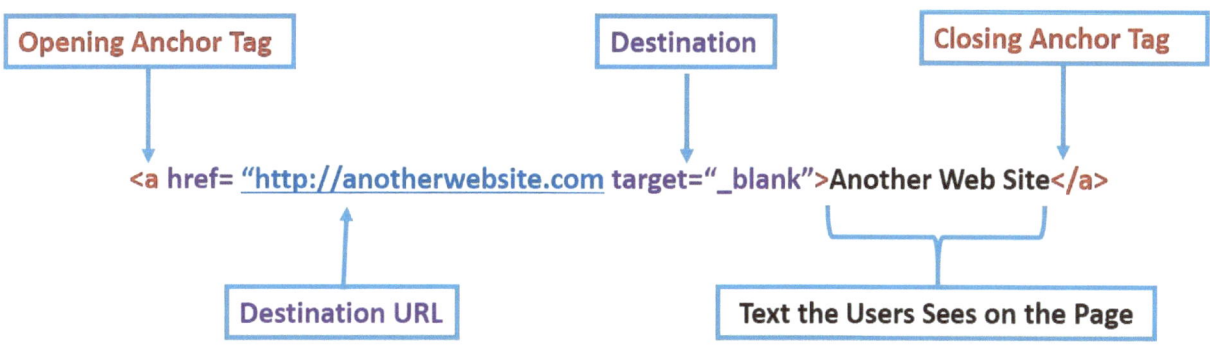

Wrapping Linked Content

A new and exciting function introduced in HTML5 is the ability to wrap content in an <a> anchor tag to maximize link area.

Creating Bookmarks with the ID Attribute

Creating a link to go to a different area in the same page is a 2-step process. First, you will need to create a unique id attribute. The Identification (id) attribute is used to create a bookmark/internal tag. For example, to create an id named tip.

<article id="tips">

The pound sign (#) is used with the id attribute to create the internal link.

<a href="#tips">

The pound sign (#), the id name, along with the page URL is used to create a bookmark to a specific place on the page of a separate URL.

<a href="html_tips.html#tips">

Image Links

<a href="thebitagroup.com/courses.asp" target="_blank"> <img src="graphic.jpg"> </a>

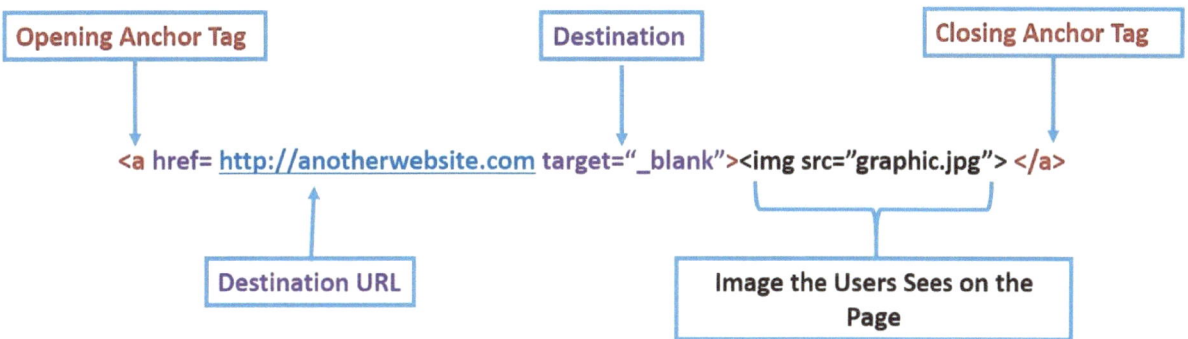

Email Links

The **address** element is used to wrap content that describes an address or contact information which may include: Physical address; Email address; Web address; Phone Numbers, etc.

In this section the email address is created using the <a> tag, the href attributes, and the mailto: property of the href attribute.

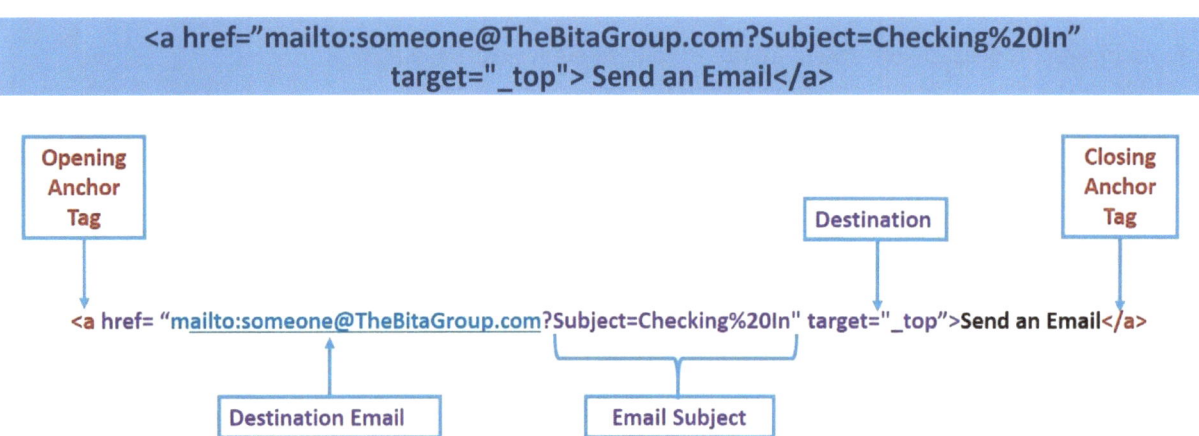

It is common to find address information in the footer sections of website, so let's take a look at an example.

```
<footer>
    <div class="webmaster">Please send any questions or issues with the site to:
      <address>
          <a title= "shere" href= "http://thebitagroup.com/contact">WEBMASTER</a>
      </address> or call between the hours of
      <time datetime= "hoo"> 9:00 A.M. – 5:00 P.M.</time>
    </div>
</footer>
```

File Links

Links used to download or open PDF, Word, Excel, etc. files are identical to the any other link you will make. Just make sure to type the extensions (.pdf, .doc, .xls, etc.) in correctly.

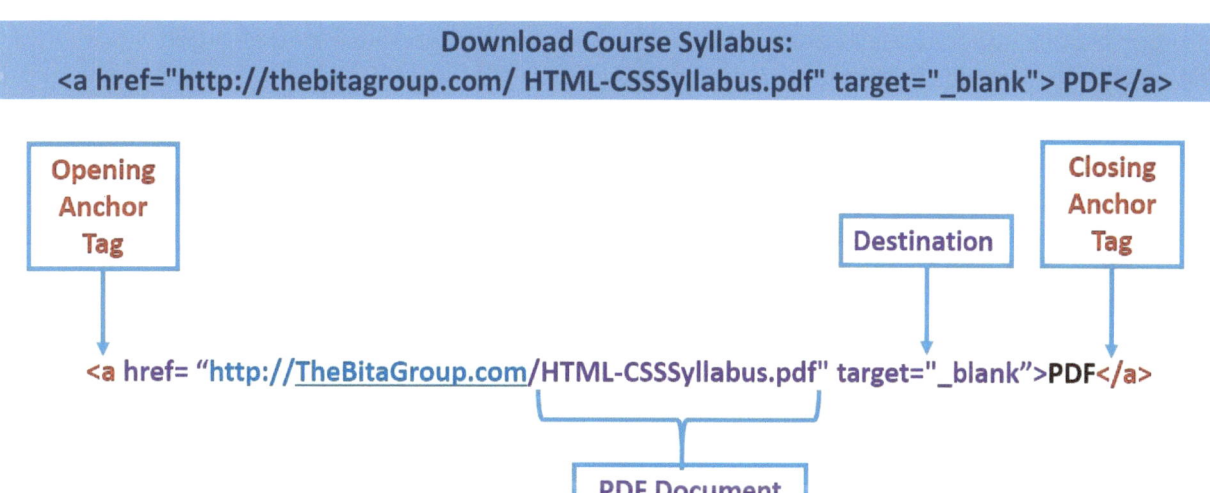

IMAGES

The web is not only a means to share information, it is a visual medium. Images on the web have always played an important role in not only the dissemination of information, but also in the design of the user interface and ways to further to engage users.

The empty <img> image element is used to place an image in the page. Like many other elements the <img> tag has required and helpful attributes that make up the full tag.

First, you will need to create the basic <img> tag, using the src (source) attribute to tell the browsers where the image resides within your remote files.

src   The location of the image.

```
<img src="image.jpg">
```

alt   The text that displays in a tooltip or if the image does not.

```
<img src="image.jpg"
     alt="tooltip">
```

height The height of the image in pixels or a percentage.

```
<img src="image.jpg"
     alt="tooltip"
     height= "#px">
```

width   The height of the image in pixels or a percentage.

```
<img src="image.jpg"
    alt="tooltip"
    height= "#px"
    width= "#px">
```

longdesc   A description of the image that will display on the page and is read to screen readers.

```
<img src="image.jpg"
    alt="tooltip"
    height= "#px"
    width= "#px"
    longdesc="description for the pages">
```

Image Compression

Media in the form of music, videos, and images are the main culprits of slow sites. Unfortunately, music and videos cannot be compressed for increased site optimization easily, but images can. Many images sizes can be decreased in size without any visual loss of quality. First, let's take a look at the most common image types:

	USE	TYPE	COLORS	SPECIALITY	COMPRESSION	SIZE
JPEG/JPG Joint Photographic Experts Group	Photograph	Raster	24-Bit	Resolution of Pixels	Lossy	Largest
GIF	Simple Graphic	Raster	256 Pixels	Fully opaque or transparent pixels Animation	Lossless	Smallest
PNG Portable Network Graphic	Complex Graphic	Raster	Millions of Pixels	8-Bit Transparency Layers	Lossless	

A **JPG** is an example of a lossy image. Photographs can undergo substantial optimization. The removal of data from the pixels of the photograph to make the file size smaller is called **Lossy** compression. Lossy compression is a permanent removal of color and thus the photograph cannot be restored back to its original state.

A **GIF** is a very small file. Compression of a gif is in most cases impossible because it is as small as it will get even after compression.

A **PNG** is another example of a lossless image. A PNG supports millions of colors and taut excellent quality It supports full transparency, the ability to set the opacity of an element within images from zero (invisible) to 100 (full visibility). Lossless compression temporarily removes some of the data from the image that can be restored at any time.

CHAPTER SEVEN: AUDIO AND VIDEO

There are many sites that require audio and/or video as a foundation for the functionality of the site while with others they supply the bells and whistles. Using audio and video is correct proportions on a site makes a big difference.

In this chapter, you will:

- Work with the audio element
- Learn how to add audio files to a Web page
- Learn how to add 3-party videos to a Web page

HTML5 has new standards for working with audio and video files. Adding audio and video you your web pages is a great way to engage users. In this chapter, you will add music files and 3rd-party (YouTube) videos to Web pages.

AUDIO AND VIDEO

Audio Element

audio   Used to play an audio file in a Web page.

`<audio>`		
Required Attributes		**Other Attributes**
source	src="filename.mp3"	**autoplay** – audio will play immediately **buffered –** which ranges of the song have buffered

type	type="audio/mp3"	**controls** – audio controls will display
		
		    ▪ volume
		    ▪ seeking
		    ▪ pause/resume playback

	type="audio/ogg"	**loop** – will repeat when complete

	type="audio/wav"	**muted** – sound will be muted
		preload – audio will load when page loads not when it is called
		
		    ▪ none
		    ▪ metaadata
		    ▪ auto
		
		Volume - 0.0 (silent) to 1.0 (loudest)

Example:

<audio src="audio.mp3" autoplay controls loop volume="0.5">

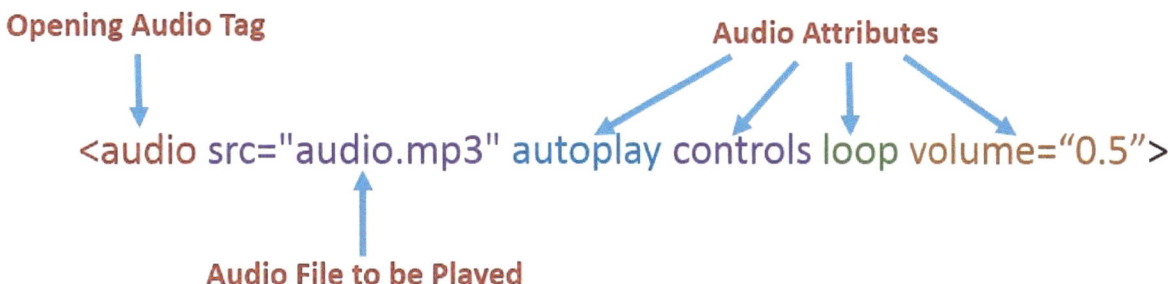

Video Element

Three basic formats for web video:

High Quality

Low Quality

High Quality

video   Used to play a video file in a Web page.

\<video\>	**\<track\>**

Required Attributes		Other Attributes
source	src="filename.mp3"	**autoplay** – audio will play immediately
type	type="audio/mp3"	**controls** – audio controls will display
		height – the height of the video display
	type="audio/ogg"	**loop** – will repeat when complete
	type="audio/wav"	**muted** – sound will be muted
		played – notes video has been previously played
		poster-URL of image for start screen
		poster="URL"
		preload – video will load when page loads not when it is called
		width – the width of the video display

Using the Embed Tag for Displaying Videos

To use a plugin such as QuickTime you would use the following:

<embed>	
Attributes	
source	src="filename.mov"
type	type="video/quicktime"
height	height="#"
width	width="#"

`<embed type="video/quicktime" src="videofile.mov" width="600" height="400">`

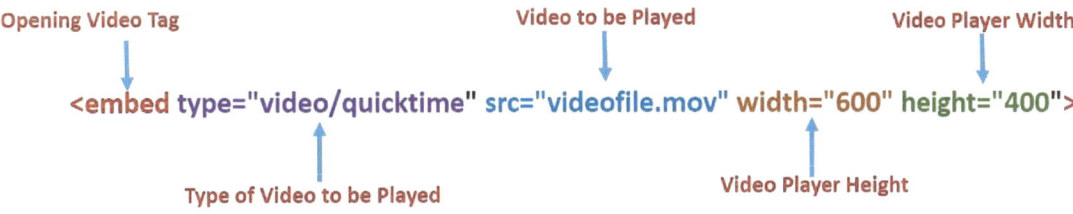

Embedding 3rd Party Videos into your Pages

Many times the video you want to display on your site has already been published to a third-party site.

You can complete this by using the embed tag and the video information supplied. For example, to embed a YouTube video into your Web pages:

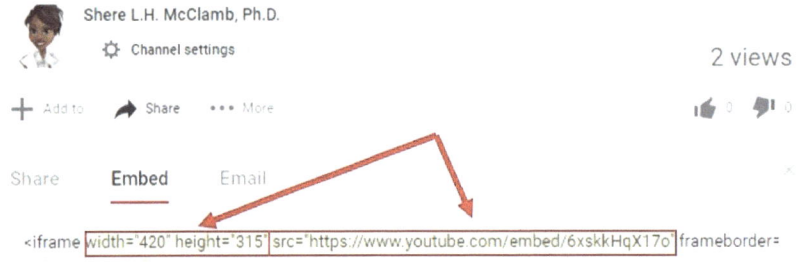

Ariannah Cooking Dinner

Shere L.H. McClamb, Ph.D.

⚙ Channel settings

2 views

➕ Add to   ➤ Share   ••• More   👍 0   👎 0

Share   **Embed**   Email

<iframe width="420" height="315" src="https://www.youtube.com/embed/6xskkHqX17o" frameborder=

CHAPTER EIGHT: BASIC TABLES

Creating basic tables in HTML range from basic to highly complicated entities existing of merged columns and rows to properly house tabular data. Let's use the table, table row, and table data elements to create basic tables.

In this chapter, you will:

- Learn to create HTML tables
- Learn to create column and row headers
- Learn how to merge table columns
- Learn how to merge table rows

The ability to create tables for your Web site will make the tasks of working with tabular data much easier. In this chapter, you will learn the elements used to create HTML tables to hold the data and information for display on your Web site.

INSERTING A TABLE

Table	<table></table>	Used to create an **HTML table**.
Table Row	<tr></tr>	Used to create a **row** in a table.
Table Data	<td></td>	Used to create a **cell** in a table.
Table Header	<th></th>	Used to create a **table header cell**.
Table Head	<thead></thead>	Used to group content as the **header** of the table.
Table Body	<tbody></tbody>	Used to group the content as the **body** of the table.
Table Footer	<tfoot></tfoot>	Used to group content as the **footer** of the table.

Border	**Thinnest Border** <table border="1">	**No Border** <table border="0">

Elements Allowed within the <table></table> Tags

Phrasing Elements	table	p	div	header	hgroup	footer	section	article
pre	address	blockquote	ins	del	hr	a	object	nav	aside
h1	h2	h3	h4	h5	h6	figure	dl	ol	ul
noscript	canvas	menu	form	fieldset	details	map	audio	video

MERGING COLUMNS AND ROWS

Colspan (Spanning Across Columns)

Information can be set to span across column using the colspan attribute. The number used should equal the number of columns the spanned td cell will cover.

<table colspan="number">

colspan="4"			

Rowspan (Spanning Across Rows)

Information can be set to span across rows using the rowspan attribute. The number used should equal the number of rows the spanned td cell will cover.

<table rowspan="number">

rowspan="3"			

<table border="1">

<tr>			
<th colspan="4" scope="col">Work Contact Points</th> **</tr>**			
<tr> **<th>**Name**</th>** **</tr>**	**<th>**Email**</th>**	**<th>**Phone**</th>**	**<th>**Office**</th>**
<tr> **<th** rowspan="3">Emp**</th>** **</tr>**	<td>Don</td>	<td>don@web.com</td>	<td>5BH</td>
	<tr> <td>Anna</td> **</tr>**	<td>anna@web.com</td>	<td>9M0</td>
	<tr> <td>Debra</td> **</tr>**	<td>debra@web</td>	<td>89K6</td>

</table>

Viewing Table Elements in the Source Code

Let's look at an example of table elements used to create a familiar web site.

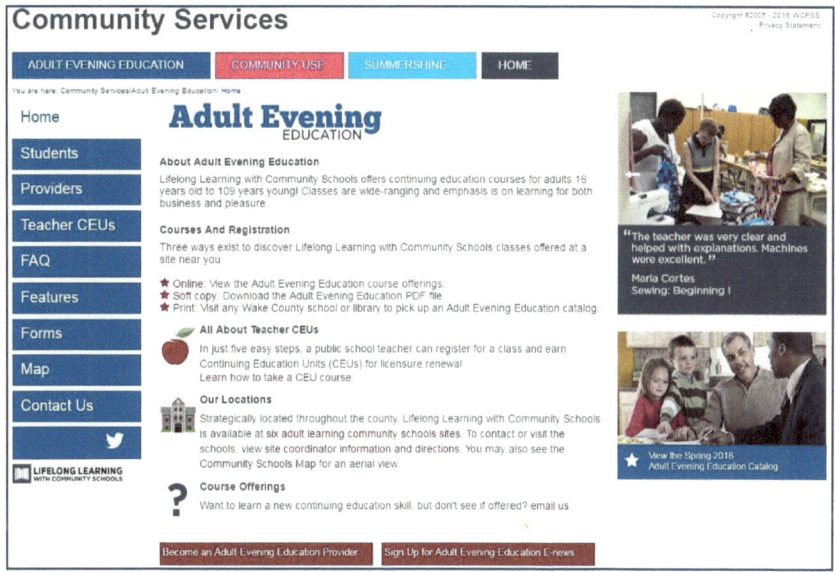

STEP 1.   Navigate to the Adult Evening Main Page
(https://cs.wcpss.net/index.php?route=lllcontroller) on the Internet.

STEP 2.   Right-Click on the page and view the source code for the page.

STEP 3.   Scroll down until you see:

<table cellpadding='0' border '0'>

Let's look at the HTML table elements and attributes used to create this table. As you see in the example there is an opening <table> tag with 3 attributes that begins the creation of the table.

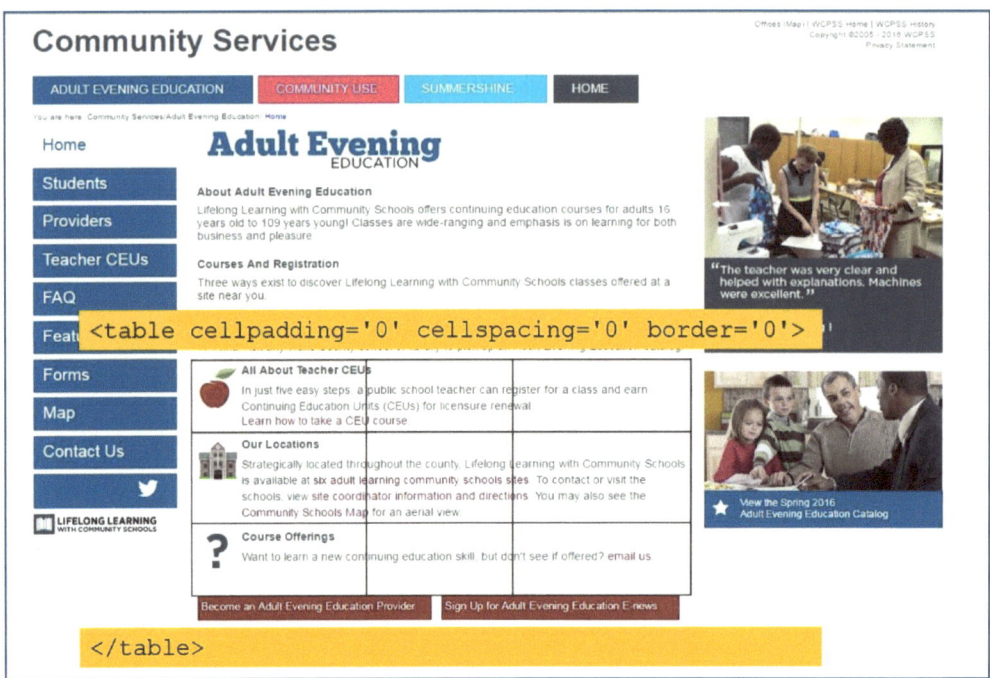

There is an ending </table> tag to let the browser no to close this table.

Creating Row 1 of the Table ….. <tr>   **Creating the Merged Cells …. <td colspan='3'>**

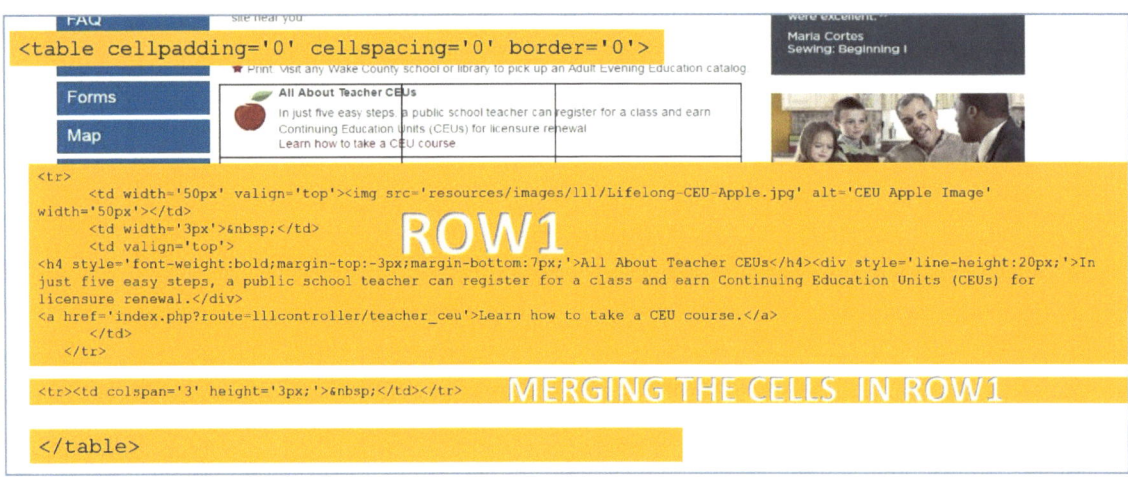

Creating Row 2 of the Table ….. `<tr>`   **Creating the Merged Cells …. `<td colspan='3'>`**

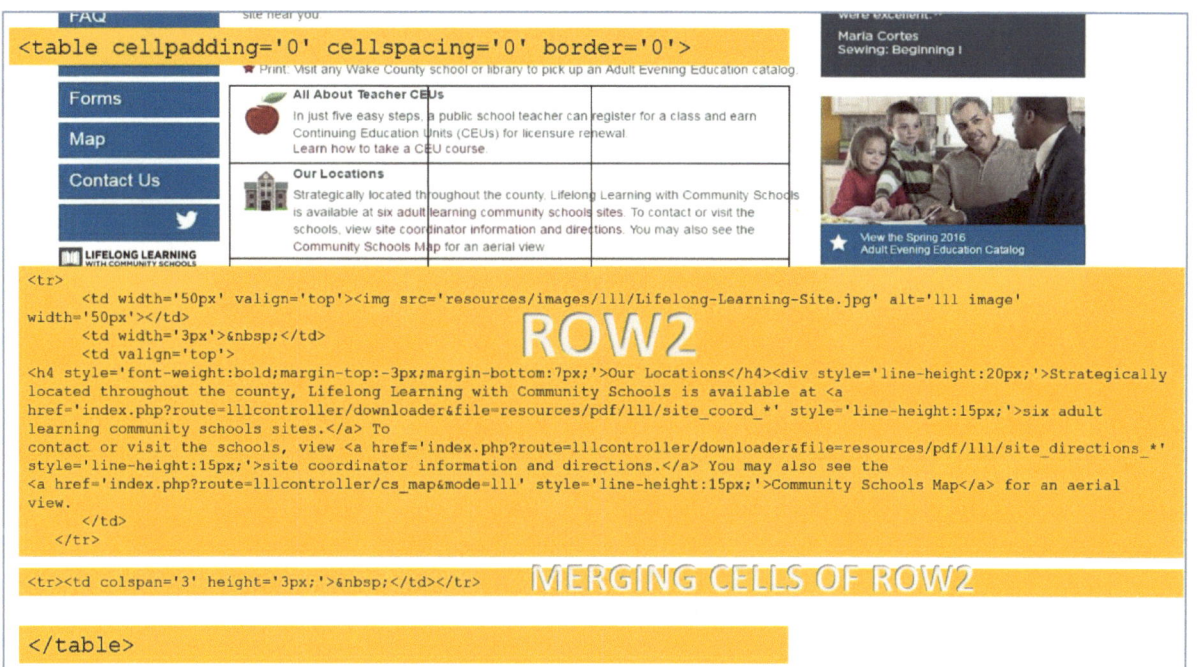

```
<table cellpadding='0' cellspacing='0' border='0'>
```

```
<tr>
     <td width='50px' valign='top'><img src='resources/images/lll/Lifelong-Learning-Site.jpg' alt='lll image'
width='50px'></td>
     <td width='3px'> </td>
     <td valign='top'>
<h4 style='font-weight:bold;margin-top:-3px;margin-bottom:7px;'>Our Locations</h4><div style='line-height:20px;'>Strategically
located throughout the county, Lifelong Learning with Community Schools is available at <a
href='index.php?route=lllcontroller/downloader&file=resources/pdf/lll/site_coord_*' style='line-height:15px;'>six adult
learning community schools sites.</a> To
contact or visit the schools, view <a href='index.php?route=lllcontroller/downloader&file=resources/pdf/lll/site_directions_*'
style='line-height:15px;'>site coordinator information and directions.</a> You may also see the
<a href='index.php?route=lllcontroller/cs_map&mode=lll' style='line-height:15px;'>Community Schools Map</a> for an aerial
view.
     </td>
   </tr>
```

ROW2

```
<tr><td colspan='3' height='3px;'> </td></tr>
```

MERGING CELLS OF ROW2

```
</table>
```

Creating Row 3 of the Table <tr>...<tr>...<tr>

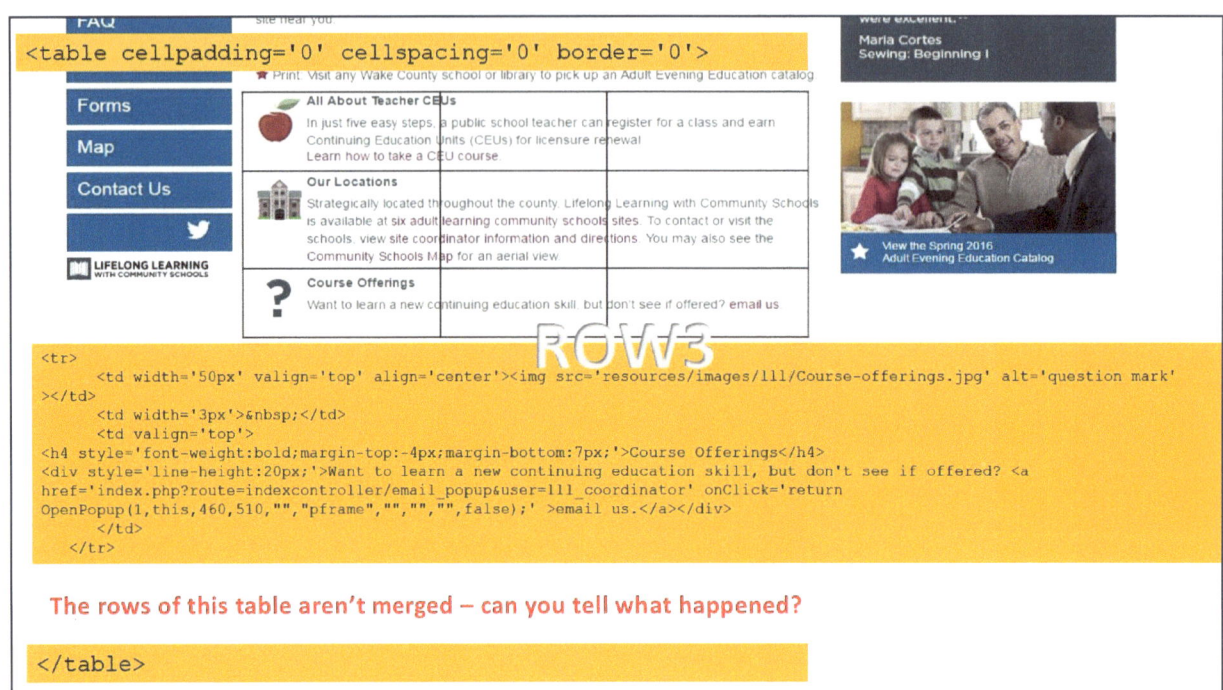

```
<table cellpadding='0' cellspacing='0' border='0'>
```

```
<tr>
    <td width='50px' valign='top' align='center'><img src='resources/images/lll/Course-offerings.jpg' alt='question mark'
></td>
    <td width='3px'> </td>
    <td valign='top'>
<h4 style='font-weight:bold;margin-top:-4px;margin-bottom:7px;'>Course Offerings</h4>
<div style='line-height:20px;'>Want to learn a new continuing education skill, but don't see if offered? <a
href='index.php?route=indexcontroller/email_popup&user=lll_coordinator' onClick='return
OpenPopup(1,this,460,510,"","pframe","","","",false);' >email us.</a></div>
    </td>
  </tr>
```

The rows of this table aren't merged – can you tell what happened?

```
</table>
```

MODULE THREE

FORMATTING WITH CASCADING STYLESHEETS (CSS 3)

CHAPTER NINE: INTRODUCTION TO CSS3

> *Welcome to Cascading Style Sheets. This is the part of the text where we start jazzing up those black and white pages you have built until now. Using CSS properties and values we will learn to format HTML structures.*

In this chapter, you will:

- Use basic CSS syntax
- Combine style rules with your HTML code
- Write your first style sheet
- Use CSS selectors to apply style rules
- Use the <span> elements with CSS rules

Even though images and videos steal the show on most web sites, text is still very important. In this chapter, you will learn to format letters, words, and sentences using CSS properties and values. You will learn basic CSS syntax and get a chance to write a variety of CSS style sheets. Berners-Lee and his colleagues realized early in the development of HTML that a style and display language, expressed separately from the structural HTML code, would let authors control the way pages were displayed on the screen.

The beauty of combining HTML and CSS is that because of the separation, each are editable without affecting the other. The use of the cascade to control the formatting of HTML documents have saved Web authors valuable time by placing the styles in separate from the content of the pages.

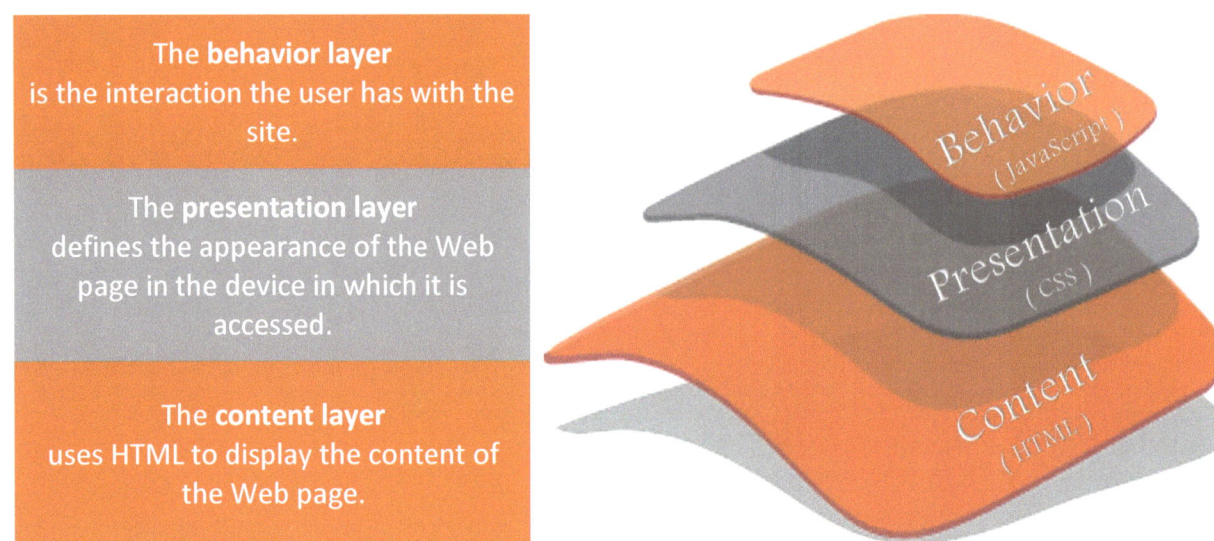

The **behavior layer** is the interaction the user has with the site.

The **presentation layer** defines the appearance of the Web page in the device in which it is accessed.

The **content layer** uses HTML to display the content of the Web page.

Even though the goal is to keep the formatting of a Web page separate from the structure, there are presentation elements (e.g. <b>, <em>, etc.) that are embedded into the document.

Cascading Style Sheets (CSS) is the best way to control the presentation layer or format the Web document in the long run. Using the cascade also allows for almost effortless changing of formatting when needed.

Property Declaration Syntax

h1 {color: red;}

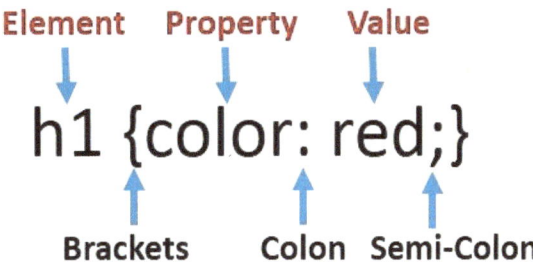

The property is a quality characteristic such as color, font-size, or margin followed by a colon. The value is the precise specification of the property, such as blue for the color, 12pt (point) for the font size, or 30px (pixels) for the margin, followed by a semicolon. CSS contains a wide variety of properties with their own set of possible values.

Types of Style

Inline styles are style added to the individual tags in the HTML document and give the least amount of control over styling the document. Internal style sheet consists of styles that reside in the webpage with the HTML formatting either within the tag as an attribute or written with the <style> tag in the head of the document. Internal styles affect only the pages in which they reside giving limited control of a set of Web pages that make up a Web site. Lastly, there are external sheets that are stand-alone documents that are shared by a number of Web pages – hence the cascade. Using an external style sheet to control many pages in the Web site is the most convenient way to control styles throughout the entire Web site.

Inline styles are created by combining the HTML elements and the style attribute. For example, if one of the H1 elements in you document should be red, you can isolate that element and give it style.

<h1>Learning CSS is Fun</h1>

<h1 style="color:red;margin-left:30px;"> Learning CSS is Fun</h1>

Opening h1 Tag

Closing h1 Tag

<h1 style="color:red;margin-left:30px;">Learning CSS is Fun</h1>

Inline Style

Internal styles are created using the <style></style> tagged pair in the head of the document. For example, if you wanted to change all of the <h2> elements in the entire document to green, you can declare it one time and the style would cascade through every instance the browser finds of that element.

```
<head>
    <style>
        h2 {
            color: green;
            }
    </style>
</head>
```

<head>

Opening Style Tag

<style>

Property   Value

h1 {color: red;}

Brackets   Colon Semi-Colon

</style>

Closing Style Tag

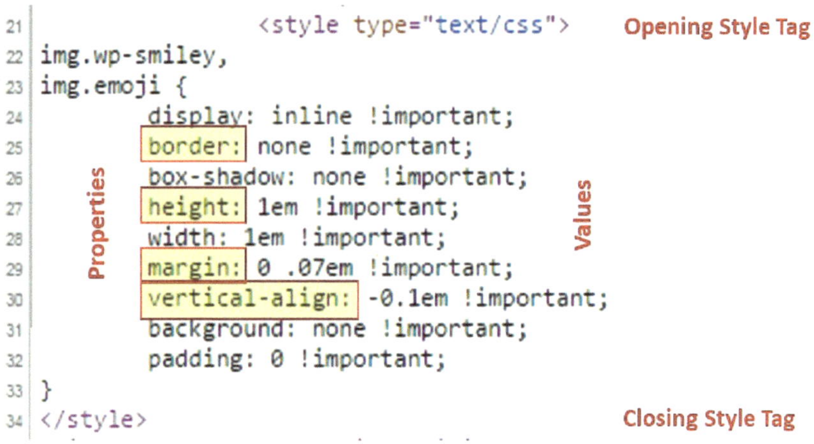

</head>

```
21              <style type="text/css">        Opening Style Tag
22  img.wp-smiley,
23  img.emoji {
24          display: inline !important;
25          border: none !important;
26          box-shadow: none !important;
27          height: 1em !important;
28          width: 1em !important;
29          margin: 0 .07em !important;
30          vertical-align: -0.1em !important;
31          background: none !important;
32          padding: 0 !important;
33  }
34  </style>                                    Closing Style Tag
```

Properties   Values

External Style Sheets are created by creating a separate document that holds the styles. For example, if you wanted to change all of the <h3> elements in the entire website to green, you can declare it one time, in one CSS document and the style would cascade through every instance the browser finds of that element in any of the pages the style sheet is linked to.

External style sheets are linked to sheets using the <link> tag.

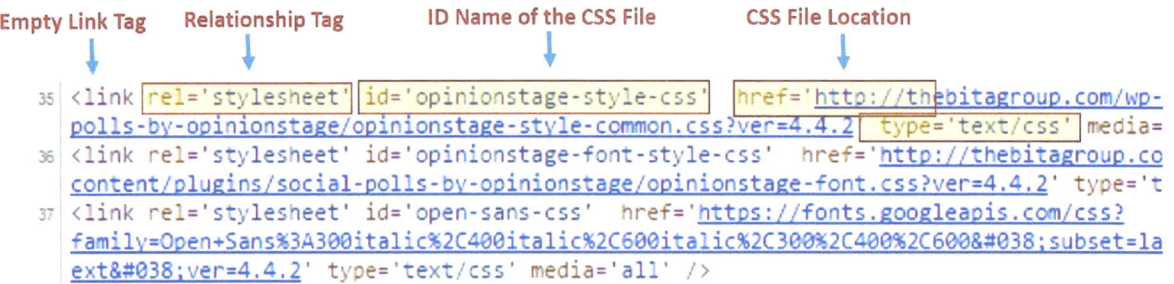

STYLING WITH COLOR

Using color is a very important skill when designing a web site. Colors are represented on the web by mixing of base colors to make others. Getting to know basic web colors:

Hexadecimal	**RGB**

- 3 sets of digits that determine the color;
- Each set stands for red, blue and green;

0 is void of color	**0** is void of color
F is full of color	**255** is full of color

BLACK = **000000** *(RED=00, GREEN=00, BLUE=00)* black = **rgb (0,0,0)** *(RED=0, GREEN=0, BLUE=0)*

white = **FFFFFF** *(RED=FF, GREEN=FF, BLUE=FF)* white = **rgb (255,255,255)** *(RED=255, GREEN=255, BLUE=255)*

Web colors are based to the amount of color the code that creates it contains. For example, the color white is VOID OF COLOR while black contains THE MOST of any other color.

Creating Basic Colors by Moving FF and 255

RED	#FF0000	rgb(255,0,0)
LIME	#00FF00	rgb(0.255.0)
BLUE	#0000FF	rgb(0,0,255)
YELLOW	#FFFF00	rgb(255,255,0)
CYAN	#00FFFF	rgb(0,255,255)
FUCSIA	#FF00FF	rgb(255,0,255)

Decoding the Numbers and Characters in Colors

00	33	66	99	CC	FF
000000	000033	000066	000099	0000CC	0000FF

Darkest to Lightest

0	51	102	153	204	255
0,0,0	0,0,51	0,0,102	0,0,153	0,0,204	0,0,255

Styling with the Color Property

The **color** property is used to add color to almost any element.

div {color: _____;}

VALUES	color name	hex color	rgb color

Styling Background's with Color

The **background-color** property is used to add space between fonts.

div {background-color: _____;}

VALUES	hex color	rgb color	transparent

Styling Borders with Color

138

The **border-color** property is used to add color to border sides.

4 Values: border-top (1)   border-right (2)   border-bottom (3)   border-left (4)

div {border-color: ____(1)____ ____(2)____ ____(3)____ ____(4)____;}

3 Values: border-top (1)   border-right and border-left (2)   border-bottom (3)

div {border-color: ____(1)____ ____(2)____ ____(3)____;}

2 Values: border-top and border-bottom (1)   border-right and border-left (2)

div {border-color: ____(1)____ ____(2)____;}

1 Value: border-top, border-bottom, border-right and border-left (1)

div {border-color: ____(1)____;}

VALUES	hex color	rgb color	transparent

The **border-top-color** property is used to add color the top border (side) of a box (see box-model)....

div {border-top-color: _____;}

The **border-right-color** property is used to add color the right border (side) of a box (see box-model).

div {border-right-color: _____;}

The **border-bottom-color** property is used to add color the bottom border (side) of a box (see box-model).

   div {border-bottom-color: _____;}

The **border-left-color** property is used to add color the left border (side) of a box (see box-model).

   div {border-left-color: _____;}

VALUES			
	hex color	rgb color	transparent

Styling Cursors with Color

The **caret-color** property is used to color the cursor on the site.

   div {caret-color: _____;}

VALUES			
	hex color	rgb color	transparent

Color Name	Hexadecimal
white	#FFFFFF
black	#FF0000
blue	#0000FF
cyan	#00FFFF
green	#00FF00
orange	#FFA500
yellow	#FFFF00
red	#FF0000

WORKING WITH BACKGROUNDS

Element	Property	Value
body {	**background-color:**	any color name or hex
	background-image:	background-image: url("awesome.jpg");
	background-repeat:	repeat | repeat-x | repeat-y | no-repeat

		left bottom	right top	center top
		left center	right center	center center
		left bottom	right bottom	center bottom
	background-position:	x% y% *(Default value: 0% 0%)* The top left corner is 0% 0%. The right bottom corner is 100% 100%. When only specify one value, the other value will be 50%.		
	background-attachment:	scroll *(default)* – scrolls with page fixed – stays still when scrolling		

STYLING LINKS

Element	Property	Value
anchor	color	any color name or hex
a:link	color	any color name or hex
a:visited	color	any color name or hex
a:hover	color	any color name or hex
a:active	color	any color name or hex

```
a {
    color: purple;
}
```

```
a:visited {
    color: purple;
}
```

```
a:hover {
    color: purple;
}
```

Removing Underlines from Links

```
a:link {
    text-decoration: none;
}
```

To Underline Links

```
a:hover {

        text-decoration: underline;

    }
```

Fancy links

```
a:link, a:visited {

        text-decoration: none;
        color: hotpink;
        padding: 15px;
        display: inline-block;

    }
```

WORKING WITH TABLES

Table Borders

When applying borders to tables by using the border property will place a border on each cell.

Add a border to your table.

```
table {
        border: 1px solid blue;
    }
```

Add a border to the cells of the table.

```
table, th, td {
        border: 2px dotted red;
    }
```

Now collapse the borders of each cell into a single border the kind we are used to seeing around tables.

```
table {
        border-collapse: collapse;
    }
```

Now add the same border to the table.

```
table, th, td {

        border: 2px dotted red;

    }
```

Let's center align the text in the header cells of the table.

```
th {

        text-align: center

    }
```

WORKING WITH SELECTORS

In this chapter, you will learn to format elements by selecting, classes, ID's, attributes, and descendants. Formatting using these selecting methods will lay a firm foundation for more complex formatting methods used in cascading style sheets. It is important to grasp and practice these methods of selection throughout the pages in your websites. CSS is a straight-forward method of formatting HTML documents. Learning CSS is an iterative process that requires attention to detail from the very first lesson.

Grouping Selectors

We have seen in the previous chapter how to create a CSS declaration using the element, property, and a value. We have also applied that declaration to an HTML element. Building on that premise, we will now apply that same style to multiple selectors using grouping.

In earlier examples, we turned the color of h1 text the color red using:

h1 {color: red; background-color: yellow;}

So, now you want all of the h1 and h3 text to be red.

You could very well type the two declarations separately to accomplish this task. An easier way to group the two selectors into one declaration. To group elements, place them, separated by a comma into one declaration. The comma that separates the two elements are very important, it tells the browser that this rule will affect two separate and different elements throughout the document.

h1, h2 {color: red; background-color: yellow;}

Let's take this a little further. What if you wanted the color of several elements throughout the document to be red?

You could of course create a declaration for each of them:

h1 {color: red; background-color: yellow;}

h2 {color: red; background-color: yellow;}

h3 {color: red; background-color: yellow;}

h4 {color: red; background-color: yellow;}

h5 {color: red; background-color: yellow;}

h6 {color: red; background-color: yellow;}

Or you could use the grouping method. This will work for any number of elements

h1, h2, p, article, address, h3, h5 {color: red; background-color: yellow;}

CSS COMMENTS

You can place comments in the CSS file that do not affect the formatting to the HTML document. Comments are used to provide documentation within the code.

```
/*

        comment text here

*/
```

If you saw this in the head of an HTML document, what would you know about this CSS code?

```
42
43      <style type='text/css'>
44        <!--
45  /*      @font-face{
46            font-family: gotham narrow book;
47            src: url(resources/styles/gothamnarrow-book.woff);
48          }
49
50          @font-face{
51            font-family: gotham book;
52            src: url(resources/styles/gotham-book.woff);
53          }*/
54
55          body {
56            margin-top:0px;
57            background-color:white;
58          }
```

Here's a hint.

```
42
43    <style type='text/css'>
44      <!--
45  /*      @font-face{
46            font-family: gotham narrow book;
47            src: url(resources/styles/gothamnarrow-book.woff);
48          }
49
50        @font-face{
51            font-family: gotham book;
52            src: url(resources/styles/gotham-book.woff);
53          }*/
54
55        body {
56            margin-top:0px;
57            background-color:white;
58          }
```

You're Right!! This internal CSS formatting has been commented out and is not in use in this document.

CHAPTER TEN: TEXT IN CSS

> *Enhancing the text of your site will go a long way to furthering the engagement of your audience. Upgrading the look and making text on your site more legible is also important to accessibility!*

In this chapter, you will:

Learn how to :

- work with text
- declare fonts
- style fonts
- space fonts

Text is the cornerstone of most sites on the web. Although it can be easily overlooked, you should not. Sometimes it can make the difference in a good site and an awesome site. The finishing touches you put into your pages may not be the first thing visitors notice, but they will make distinctions between a well-designed and formatted site and one that is not. Let's get started providing you with the tools to continue to make your WordPress Web Site Awesome.

WORKING WITH TEXT

Horizontal Alignment

Horizontally aligning text in CSS is achieved using the **text-align** property.

<div style="text-align: _____;">

VALUES	left	center	right	justify

Vertical Alignment

Vertically aligning text in CSS is achieved using the **vertical-align** property.

style="vertical-align: _____;">;

VALUES	bottom	middle	top	**text**-bottom
	text$_{sub}$	baseline	text^{super}	**text-top**

Word Spacing

The **word-spacing** property is used to specify the space between words.

p {word-spacing: _____px;}

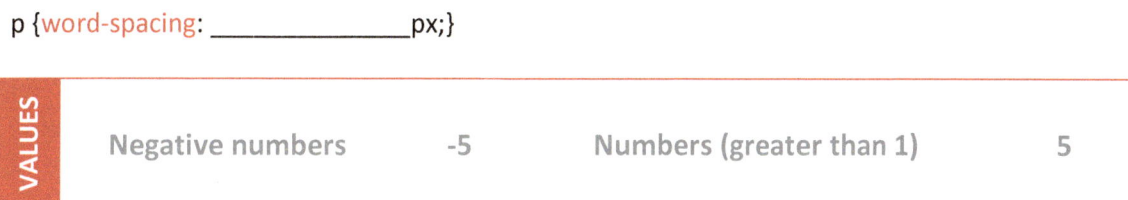

VALUES			
Negative numbers	-5	Numbers (greater than 1)	5

Wrapping Text

The **word-wrap** property is used to break words to the next line of text.

p. name {word-wrap: break-word;}

VALUES			
normal *break words only at allowed break points*	**break-word** *unbreakable words are broken*	initial	inherit

Line Height

The line-height property is used to specify the space between lines.

p. {line-height: _____;}

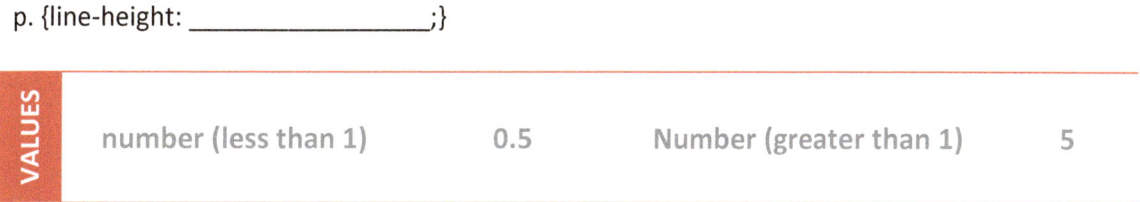

VALUES			
number (less than 1)	0.5	Number (greater than 1)	5

Shadowing Text

The **text-shadow** property is used to highlight or shadow text.

h1 {text-shadow: _____px _____px #_____;}

| VALUES | h-shadow
required | v-shadow
required | blur-radius
optional | color
optional |

Decorating Text

The **text-decoration** property is used to set or remove decorations from text.

a {text-decoration: _____;}

| VALUES | none | overline | line-through | underline |

Indenting Text

The **text-indent** property is used to specify the indentation of the first line of a text.

p {text-indent: _____px;}

| VALUES | positive number | 5 | negative number | -5 |

Transforming Text

The **text-transform** property is used to specify uppercase and lowercase letters in a text.

p.*name* {text-transform: uppercase;}

VALUES			
	uppercase	lowercase	capitalize

Spacing Words

The **word-spacing** property is used to increase or decrease the amount of space between words.

p {word-spacing: _____px;}

VALUES				
	positive number	5	negative number	-5

Adding White Space

The **white-space** property is used to handle content that has run out of space within its element.

div {white-space: _____; overflow: hidden; text-overflow: ellipsis;}

VALUES					
	normal	nowrap	pre	pre-line	pre-wrap

Overflow

The **overflow** property is used to handle content that has run out of space within its element.

div {white-space: nowrap; overflow: _____; text-overflow: ellipsis;}

| visible | hidden | scroll | auto |

Overflowing Text

The **text-overflow** property is used to handle content that has run out of space within its element.

div {white-space: nowrap; overflow: hidden; text-overflow: _____;}

| clip | ellipsis | string |

STYLING FONTS

Sizing Fonts

The **font-size** property is used to specify the size of the fonts on the site.

div.name {font-size: _____px;}

VALUES

A Number Value
Positive or Negative

div.name {font-size: _____%;}

VALUES

A Number Value
= 1% to 100% of the parent element

div.name {font-size: _____;}

VALUES

A Word Value
xx-small, x-small, small, medium (default), large, larger, x-large, xx-large

Font-Weight

The **font-weight** property is used to add or subtract weight from a font.

div.name {font-weight: _____%;}

A Number Value
100 to 900 of the parent element
400 is normal – 700 is bold

div.name {font-weight: _____;}

A Word Value
lighter, normal, bold, bolder

Font-Style

The **font-style** property is used to add a style to a font.

div.name {font-style: _____;}

normal   italic   oblique

Font-Variant

The **font-variant** property is used to add a style to a font in small caps.

div.name {font-variant: _____;}

VALUES		
	normal	small-caps

FONT SPACING

Kerning (Font Spacing)

The **font-kerning** property is used to add space between fonts.

div {font-kerning: _____;}

auto   normal   none

Kerning (Spacing Letters)

The **letter-spacing** property is used to adds or subtracts space between letters.

div {letter-spacing: _____px;}

A Number Value
Positive or Negative

DECLARING FONTS

Using @charset

The **@charset** property is used to specify the character set or the set of characters that will be used to create text on the site.

   @charset "charset";

Using @font-face

The **@font-face** property is used to specify the fonts to be used and how they will be look on the site.

   @font-face {font-family: _____; src: url(_____);}

DESCRIPTORS	font-family	src	font-stretch	font-style	font-weight
	name	*URL*	*normal, condensed, ultra-condensed, extra condensed, expanded, semi-expanded, extra-expanded, ultra-expanded*	*normal, italic, oblique*	*normal, bold 100 to 900*

Choosing a Family of Fonts for the Site or Element

The **@font-family** property is used to specify the fonts to be used on the site in the order they are listed and available.

   p {font-family: "Times New Roman", Times, serif;}

VALUE	generic family names	generic names
	arial, courier, times	*cursive, fantasy, serif, sans-serif*

Thanks

Thank you for allowing me to guide you through your first of many journeys through the using HTML and CSS alongside the WordPress content management system to produce engaging web sites. Please look to my books and training to assist you in the future!

Dr. Shere L.H. McClamb

Shere L.H. McClamb | ShereMcClamb.com | smcclamb@gmail.com

www.ingramcontent.com/pod-product-compliance
Lightning Source LLC
Chambersburg PA
CBHW041417050326
40689CB00002B/544